GAS BOOK 18

H5

CONTENTS

H5
SHORT HISTORY

H5はまるで幾何学のようだ。多様性に溢れている。

H5は集合体であり、短期のプロジェクトから長期のものまで、様々なコラボレーションを織り成している。

H5の創始者ルドヴィック・ウプランは、アントワンヌ・バルドゥ・ジャッケと共に、初のビデオ作品であるアレックス・ゴファー『The Child』、ゼブダ『Oualalaradime』、プレイグループ『Number One』等を制作する。その後、隣人のミュージシャン、エティエンヌ・ドゥ・クレシーのアルバム『Super Discount』のジャケット作成依頼を受ける。これを機に、彼の兄弟エルヴェがH5に加わる。彼らはこのジャケットの中に、モノクローム、タイポグラフィー、ミュージシャンの顔写真の不在といった彼らのクリエイティビティの構成要素を融合させた。

1999年、ある人物がH5のオフィスを訪れ、アレックス・ゴファーやコスモ・ヴィットリらと頻繁に打ち合わせをしていた。その人物が、タイポグラフィーと印刷のスペシャリスト、ラシェル・キャザダモンで、当初2か月の予定でここに働いていたが、現在も在籍しており、H5で重要なパートを占めている。

アントワンヌが去った2001年、H5はRSA(リドリー・スコット・アソシエイツ)と契約する。この契約のもと、ルドヴィックとエルヴェはMTVアウォードを受賞したロイクソップのビデオをはじめ、マッシヴ・アタックやオーディオブリーズ、ゴールドフラップ等のビデオクリップを制作する。

グラフィックデザイナーのヨルゴ・トゥルーパスは、以前、H5のオフィスの裏手に、彼専用の作業空間を構えていた。『Magazine』に代表される独創的なビジュアルが生み出されたのは、ここの空間からだった。その頃彼は、既に雑誌『Intersection』の構想を練っていた。

フランソワ・アロークスは、現在この作業空間を引き継ぎ、使用している。ルドヴィックとエルヴェと共同で、ビデオの制作に取り組んでいる。

今日は、次のプロジェクトの打ち合わせをフルール・フォルチュネとエマニュエル・コスュとするため、ル・トンヌが訪れた。

H5は今も交流の場となっている。アポイントの有無にかかわらず、それぞれが色々な目的でここを訪れる。月曜日締め切りのプロジェクトの打ち合わせに来る者もいれば、プロ・エボリューション・サッカー4のリターンマッチをしに来る者もいる。あるいはただ挨拶のために顔を出す者もいる。

H5 is all about geometry. Variable.

H5 is a collective: a mix of one-off and long-term collaborations.

Ludovic Houplain, its founder, signed his first videos with Antoine Bardou-Jacquet (Alex Gopher's "The Child", Zebda's "Oualalaradime", Playgroup's "Number One"...). The team was soon joined by Hervé de Crécy, while his brother, the musician (and neighbour) Etienne's "Super Discount" provided the opportunity for making a record sleeve that synthesised H5's creative components: monochrome, typographic, the absence of faces...

Back then (1999), one would often bump into Alex Gopher or Cosmo Vitelli when visiting the H5 office. Rachel Cazadamont, specialised in all that's typographic and print, was initially meant to work with the collective for two months; she's still here today, and an integral part of the team.

In 2001, Antoine left H5; H5 signed with RSA (Ridley Scott Associates) and, within that structure, Ludovic and Hervé directed videos for Royksöpp (winner of an MTV Award), Massive Attack, Audiobullies and Goldfrapp.

Graphic designer Yorgo Tloupas used to have his work-space right at the back of the office, in a part separated from the rest (which is open space). That's where he created the visual identity of – amongst others – "Magazine"; at the time, he was already planning the magazine "Intersection".

It's François Alaux who's in that work-space now. He co-directs videos with Ludovic and Hervé.

Today, Le Tone dropped by for a chat with Fleur Fortuné and Emmanuel Cossu to talk about projects to come.

H5 is still a place of exchange. People drop by, with or without a rendez-vous, for the project that just has to be finished by Monday, for a chance to play a revenge-match of Pro Evolution Soccer 4, or just to say hello.

 Photo: Cecily Rozier-Chabert

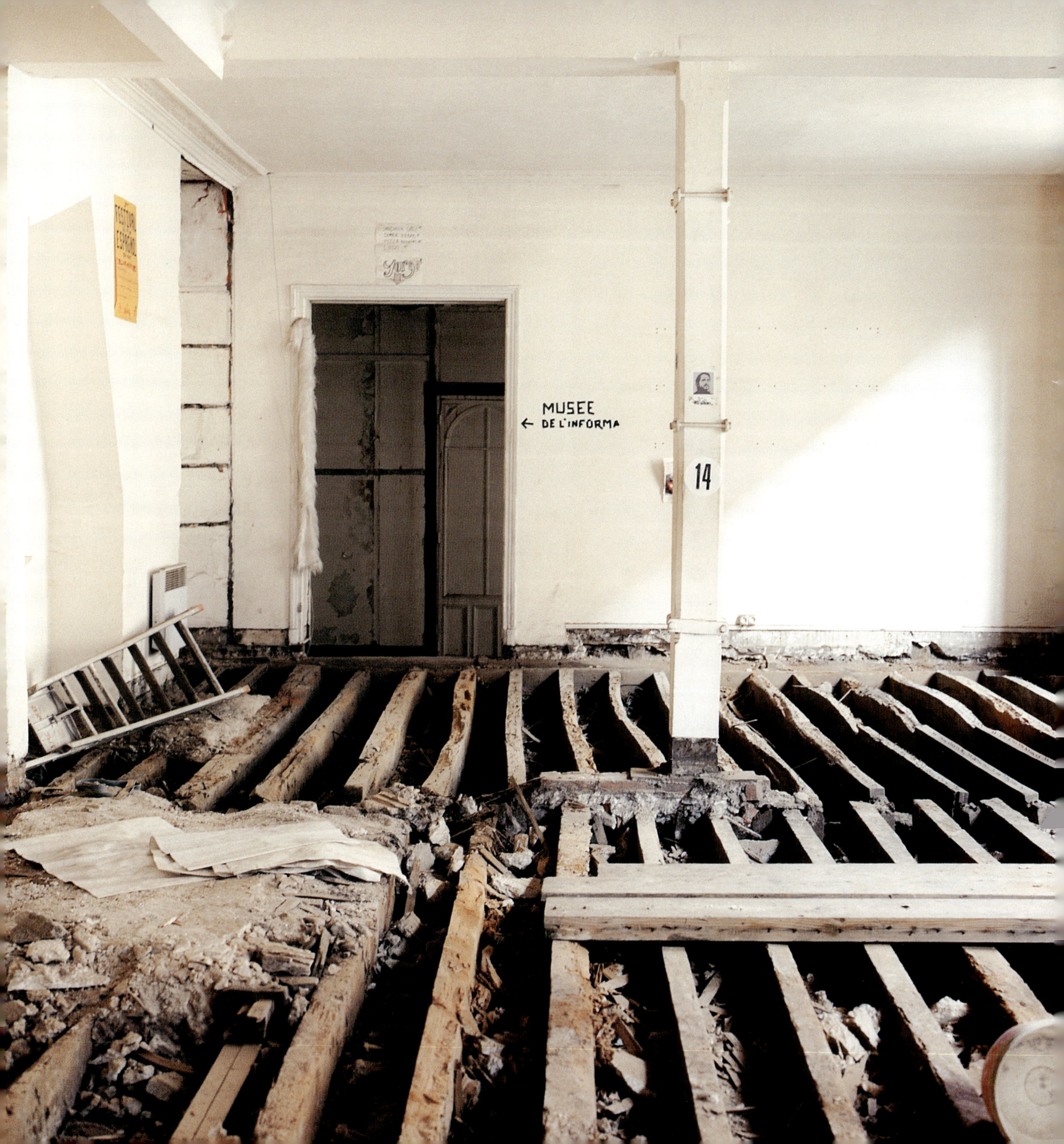

MUSEE
← DE L'INFORMA
14

REPRESENTATIVE IMAGE

文字のみを使用した、ごくシンプルで衝撃的なデザイン。しかし、このミニマルなスタイルを形成する要因は他にもある。まずエレクトロという音楽においては、歌い手や演奏者はもはや前面に打ち出される存在ではないということ。ちょうどシャンソンや歌謡曲による伝統的なイメージとは対照的である。また、写真撮影に予算が当てられないという別の要因も隠されているが。

今でもエレクトロを現代のバックグラウンドミュージックとみなす者はまだいる。エティエンヌ・ドュ・クレシーは、このような否定的な意見を逆手に取り、誰もがアクセスでき、安価で、訴求力のあるものを代表している言葉をアルバム名に選んだ―『スーパーディスカウント（SUPER DISCOUNT）』―。H5によるアルバムのグラフィックは常識破りのものだった。まるで小売り業者が用いるようなグラフィック。蛍光カラー、単色の下地に、遠くからでもはっきりと読めるシンプルなタイポグラフィー。

H5のグラフィックライティングは、流行を無視した普遍的なタイポグラフィーによる暗示的なミニマリズムを特徴としている。6年後に制作された『スーパーディスカウント2』も、蛍光ピンクの背景色を使用し、スタイルは引き続き保持された。

The image is simple, pared down; in a word, striking. But this minimalism conceals much more: the fact that electro no longer puts the singer or musicians to the forefront, in contrast with the imagery traditionally associated with “la chanson française”. Of course, another factor is that there wasn't always a budget available to pay for a photo-shoot.

Some still think of electro as modern-day muzak: Etienne de Crécy plays off this accusation and opts for a name that represents all that's most accessible, least expensive and most appealing: Super Discount. The graphics are a subversion of existing codes – those of the retail industry: a striking one-colour background that's almost fluorescent and simple typography that can be read from a long way off are used.

Much of H5's writing is summed up here: a significant minimalism that ignores typography that may be fashionable at the time of doing the work, and the choice of something that won't go out of fashion. “Super Discount 2” uses the same principle, on a background that's fluorescent pink, six years after the first album.

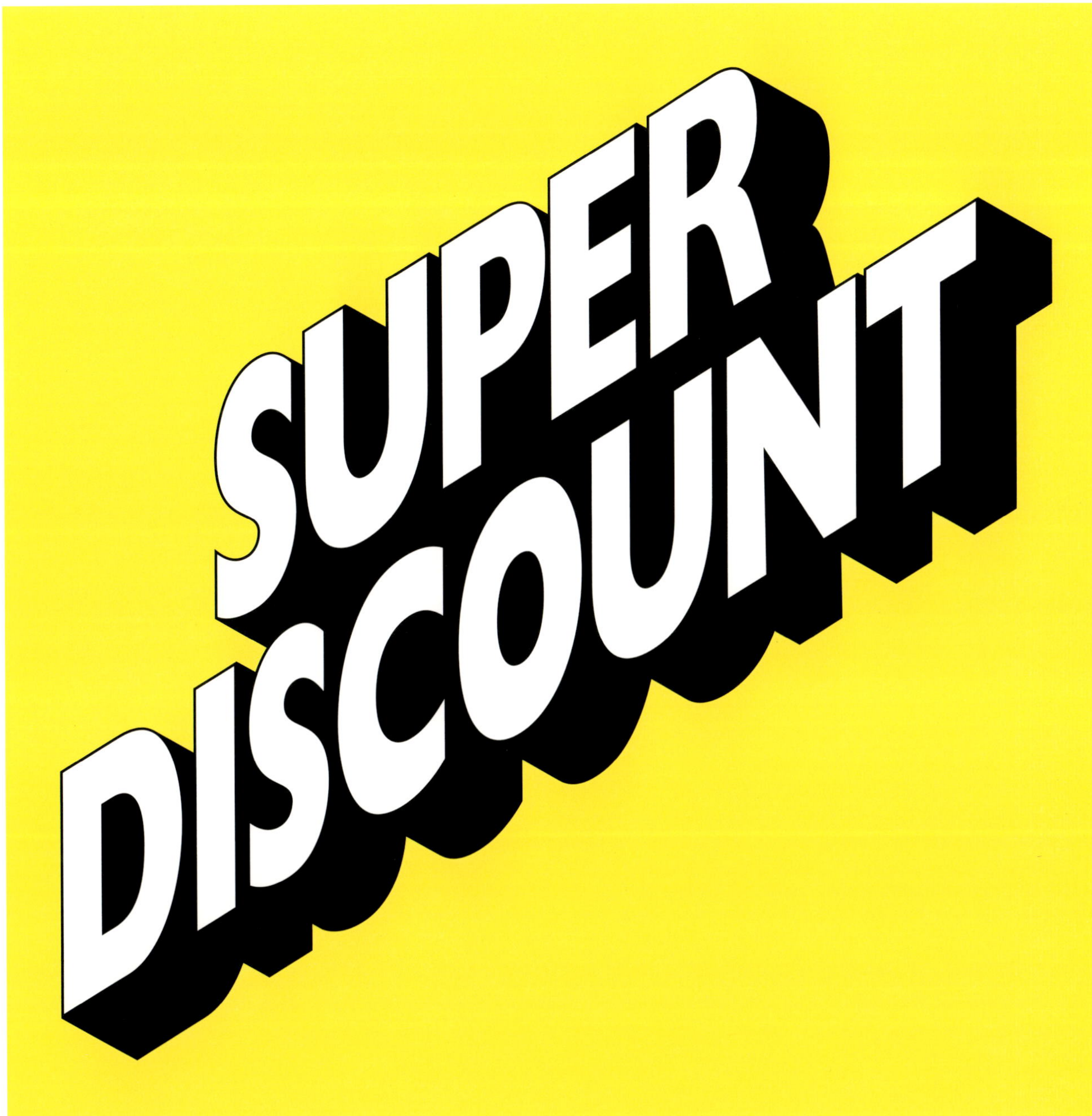

SUPER DISCOUNT 1998 Etienne de Crécy's "Super Discount" album

CHAPTER 01
WHY "ACTION !" ?

なぜ "アクション !" なのか

答え: 印刷現場での経験やアニメーションの見地から、H5は異なる種類のグラフィック言語を混在させるようになり、アニメーションをグラフィックとフィルムとの間の架け橋のようにとらえている。

WHY "ACTION !" ?

ANSWER: With a practical experience in print and a background in animation, H5 remixes different kinds of writings and considers animation like a bridge between graphics and film.

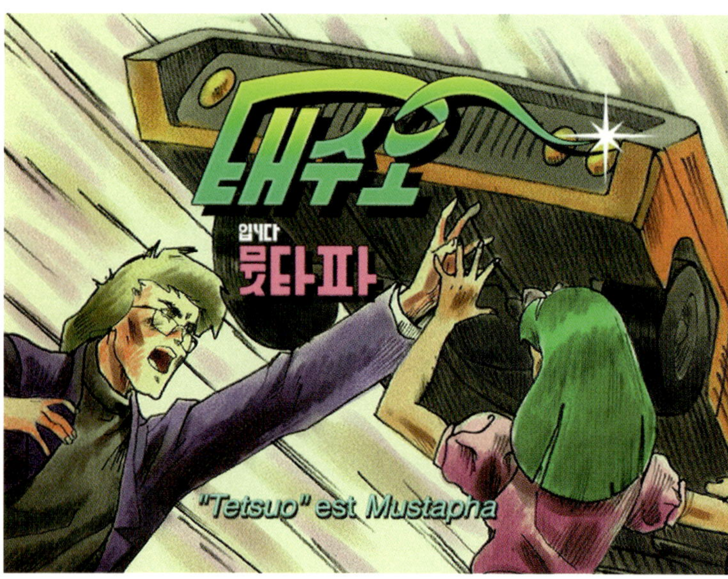

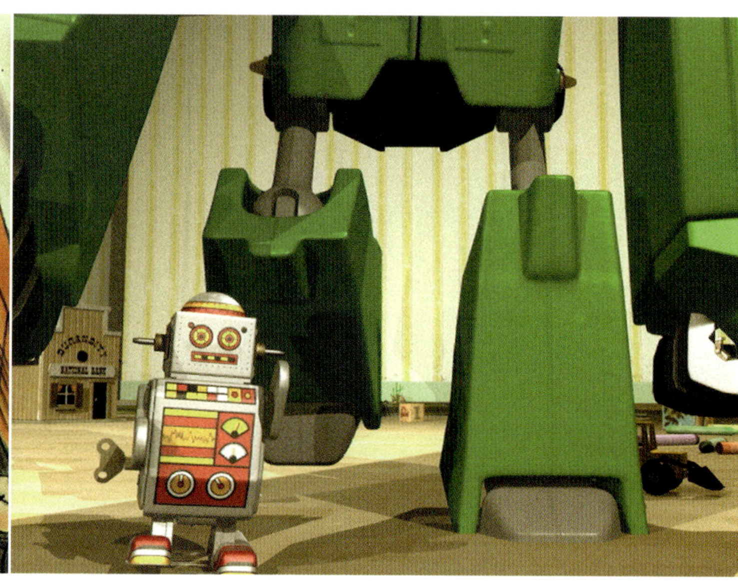

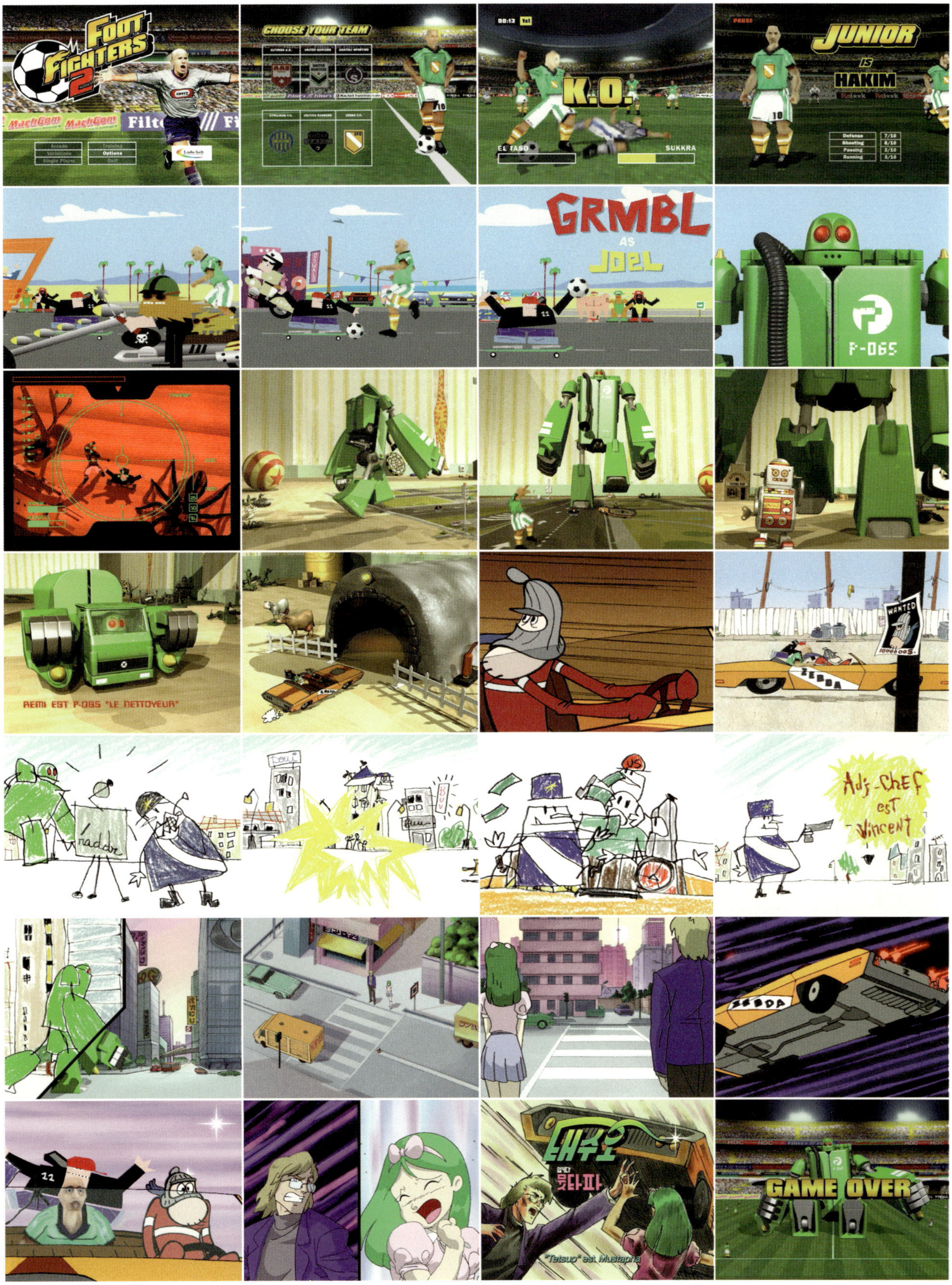

"OUALALARADIME" BY ZEBDA / Video stills from pop-promo 2000

Director: H5
Production: Partizan
Post Production: Duran
Labels: Barclay

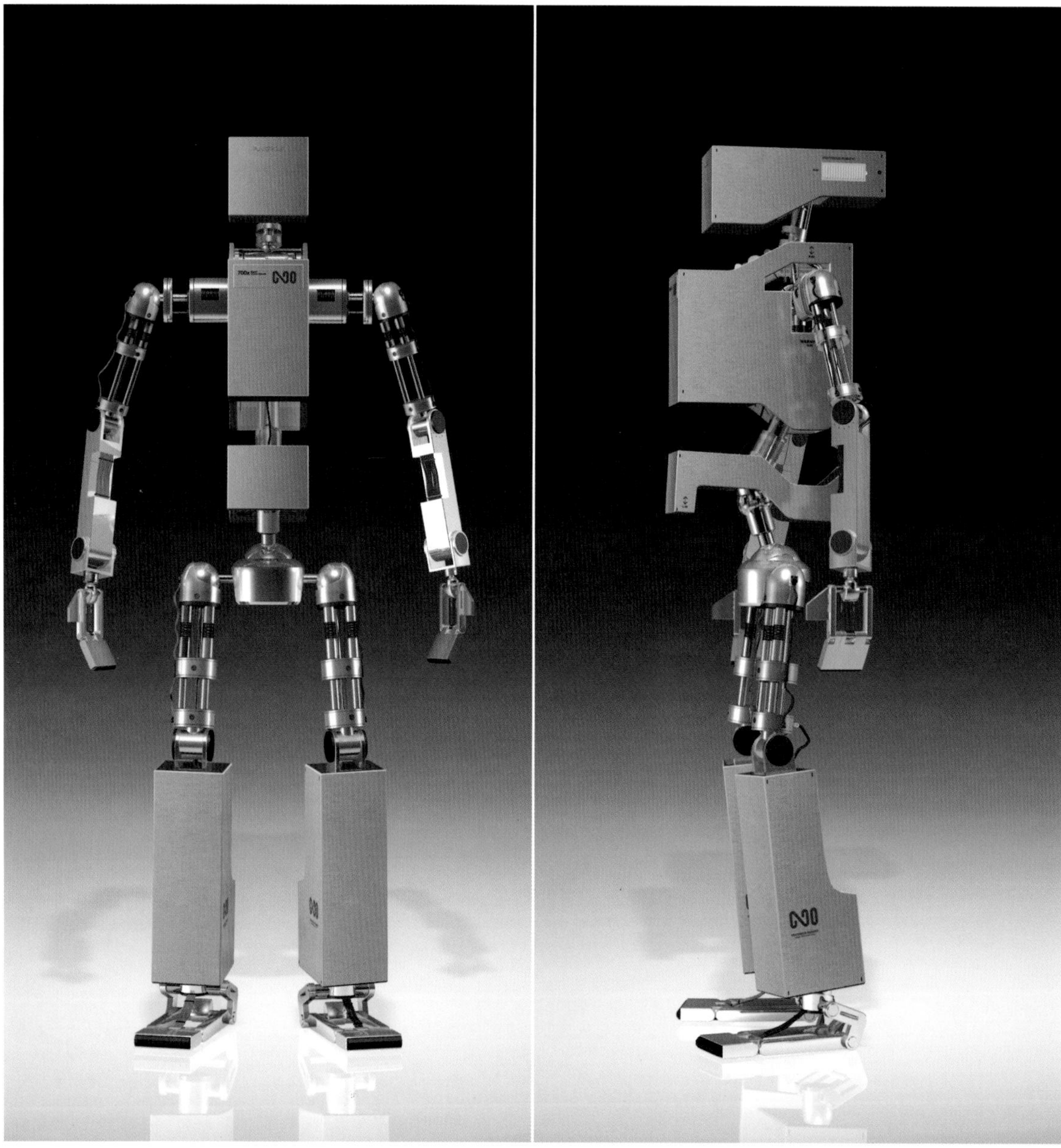

"NUMBER ONE" BY PLAYGROUP / Video stills from pop-promo 2001

Director: H5
Production: Partizan
Post Production: Duran
Labels: Source UK

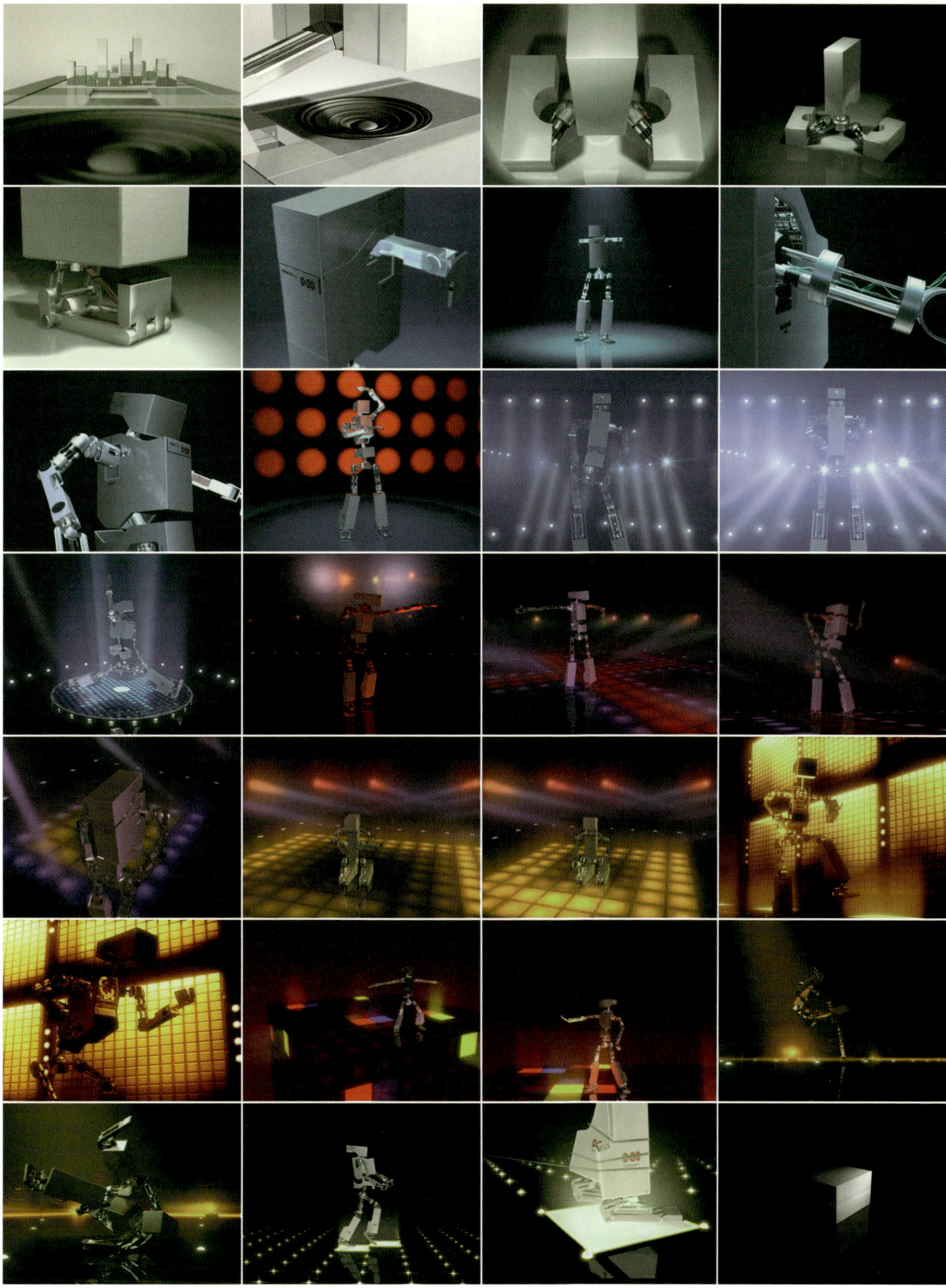

CHAPTER 02 WHY BLACK & WHITE + RED?

なぜ白黒プラス赤なのか

答え: 無駄を省くという意味もあるし、ポスター理論とも関係している。ビジュアルの効率性と即座の可読性のみを重視する。この２つの要素は、H5によって繰り返される、ライトモチーフでもある。

WHY BLACK & WHITE + RED?

ANSWER: It's to do with an economy of means, and brings to mind posterism. It is a pared down way of working that forces one to have both visual efficiency and immediate readability. It is also a recurrent combination employed by the collective, a sort of leitmotif.

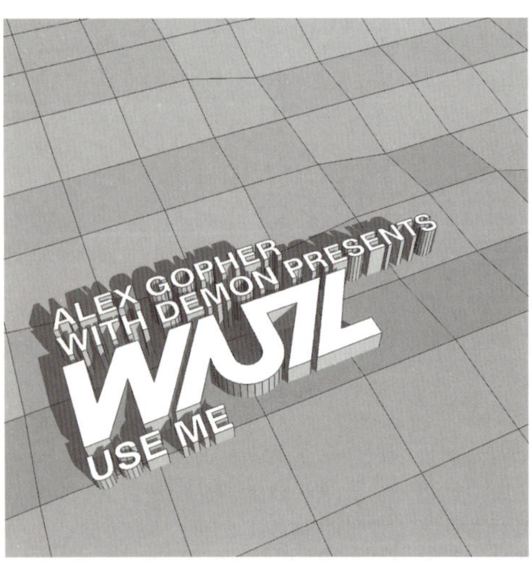

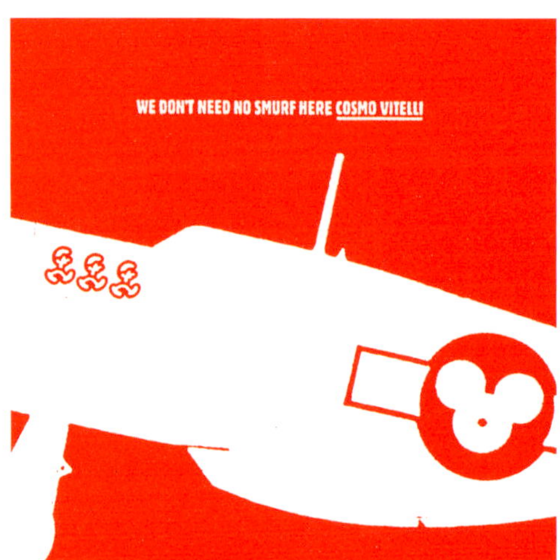

Left)	WUZ / USE ME. CD SINGLE	2001	V2 / DISQUES SOLID
Right)	COSMO VITELLI / WE DON'T NEED NO SMURF HERE. CD Single	1998	V2 / DISQUES SOLID

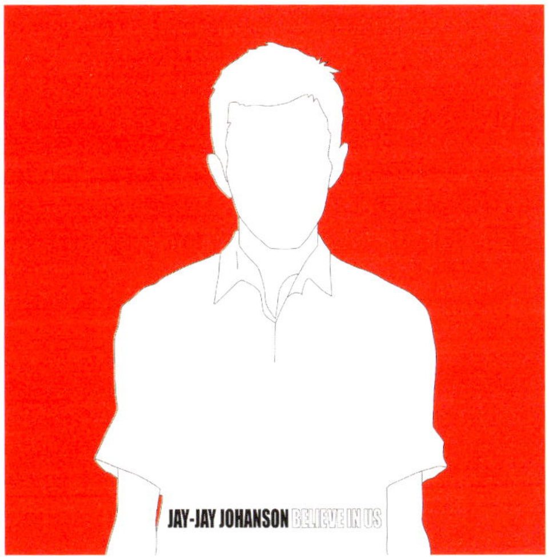

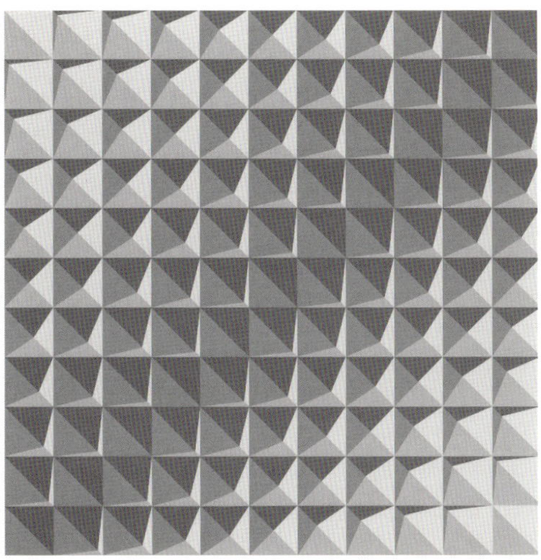

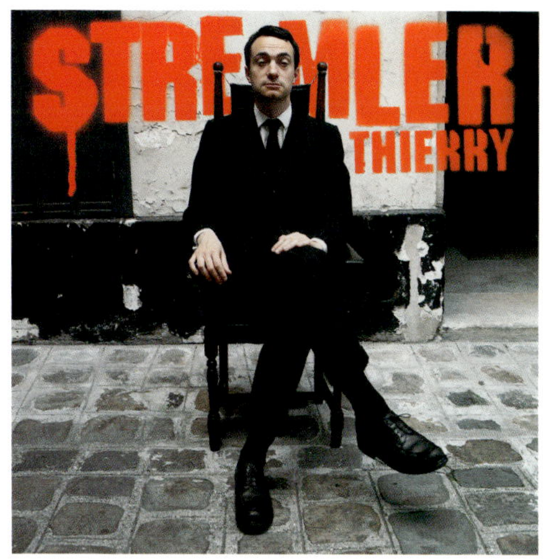

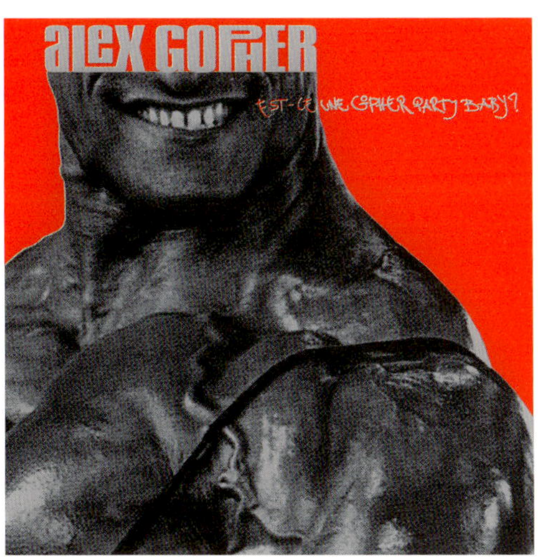

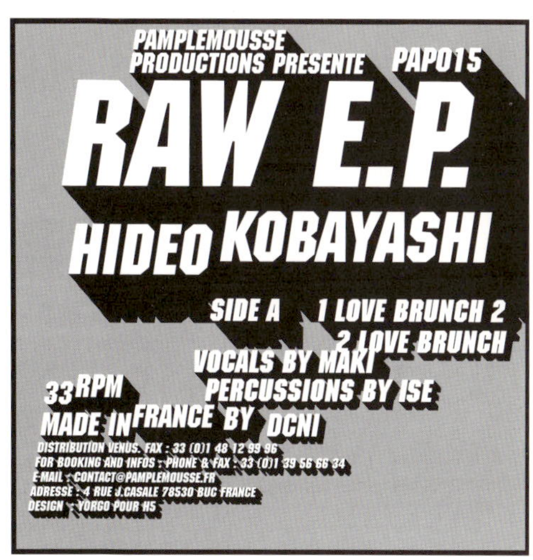

Top Left)	JAY JAY JOHANSSON / BELIEVE US. CD Single	2002	BMG
Top Right)	DIOR SOLITAIRE / EP	2001	Dior Homme / Benjamin Diamond
Middle Left)	MISTER J / RIDE EXQUIS. EP	2004	MISSIVE
Middle Right)	THIERRY STREMLER / TOUT EST RELATIF. CD Album	2001	SOURCE / DISQUES SOLID
Bottom Left)	ALEX GOPHER / EST-CE UNF GOPHER PARTY BABY ?. CD Single	1996	V2 / DISQUES SOLID
Bottom Right)	HIDEO KOBAYASHI / RAW. EP	2001	PAMPLEMOUSSE

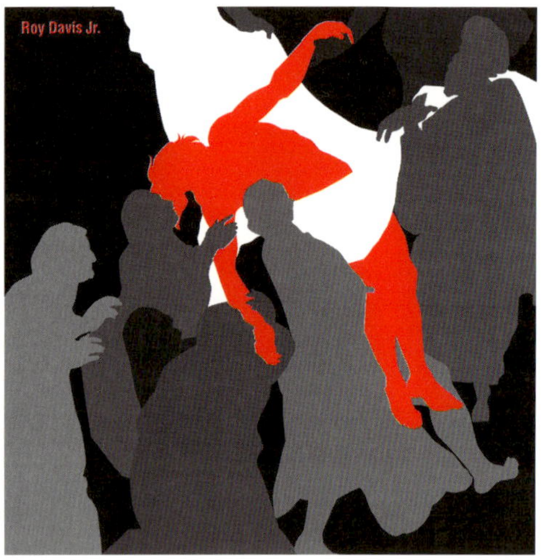

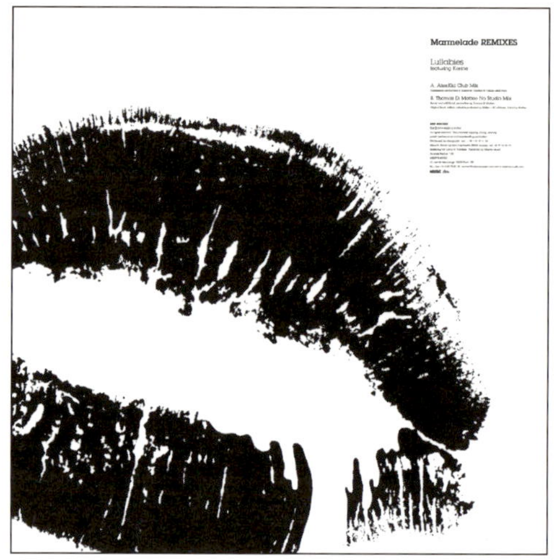

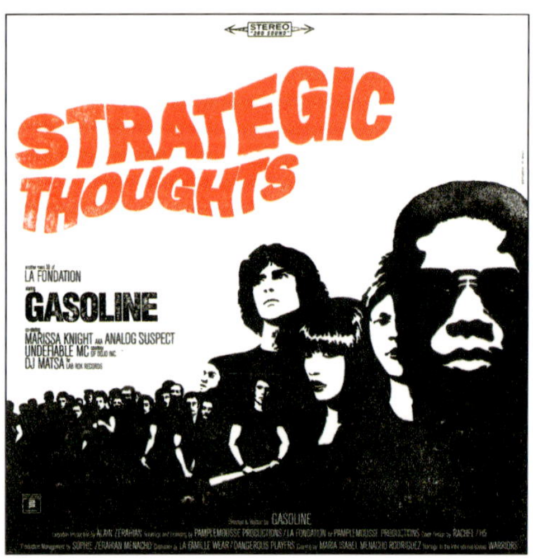

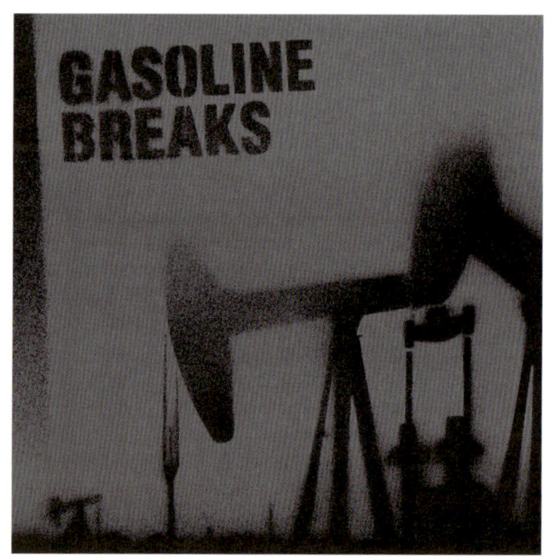

Top Left) ROY DAVIES JR / JOIN HIS KINGDOM. EP 2000 20000ST
Top Right) LULLABIES / MARMELADE REMIXES. EP 2004 MISSIVE
Bottom Left) GASOLINE / STRATEGIC THOUGHTS. EP 2004 LA FONDATION
Bottom Right) GASOLINE BREAKS / GASOLINE BREAKS. EP 2003 LA FONDATION

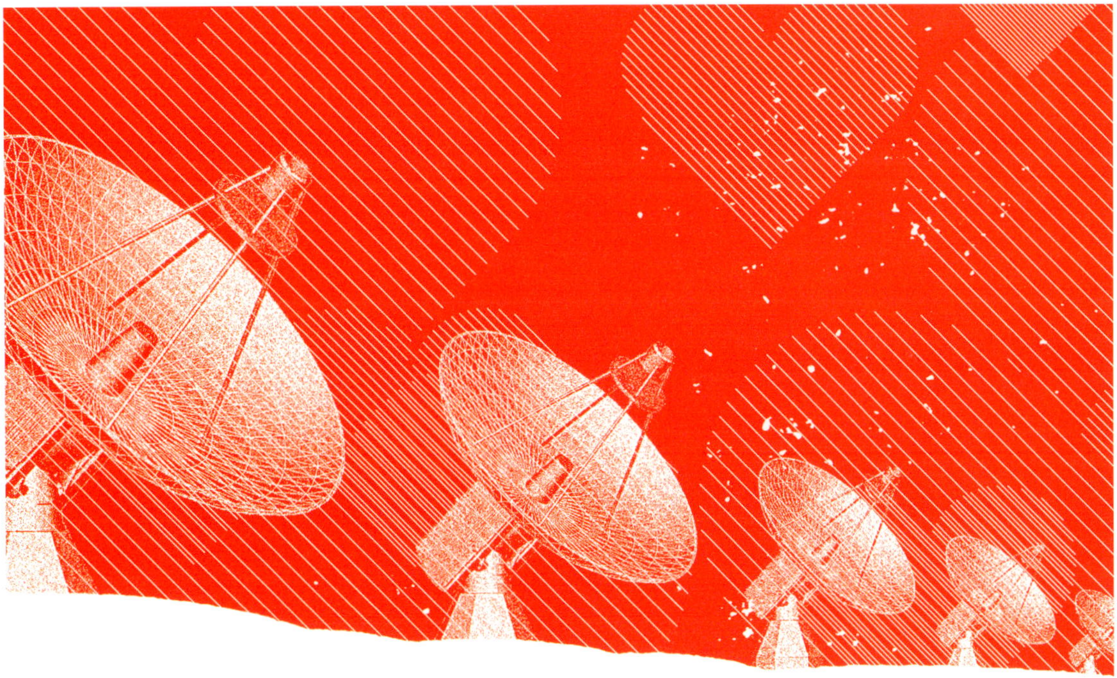

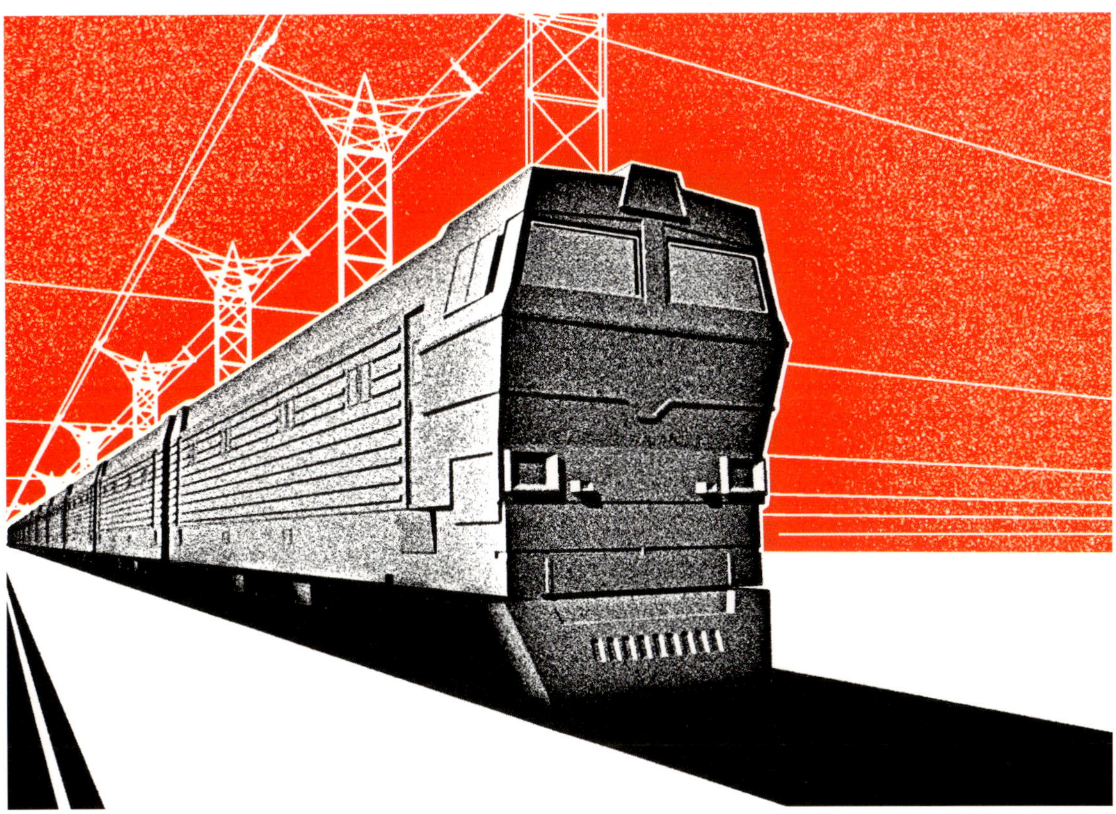

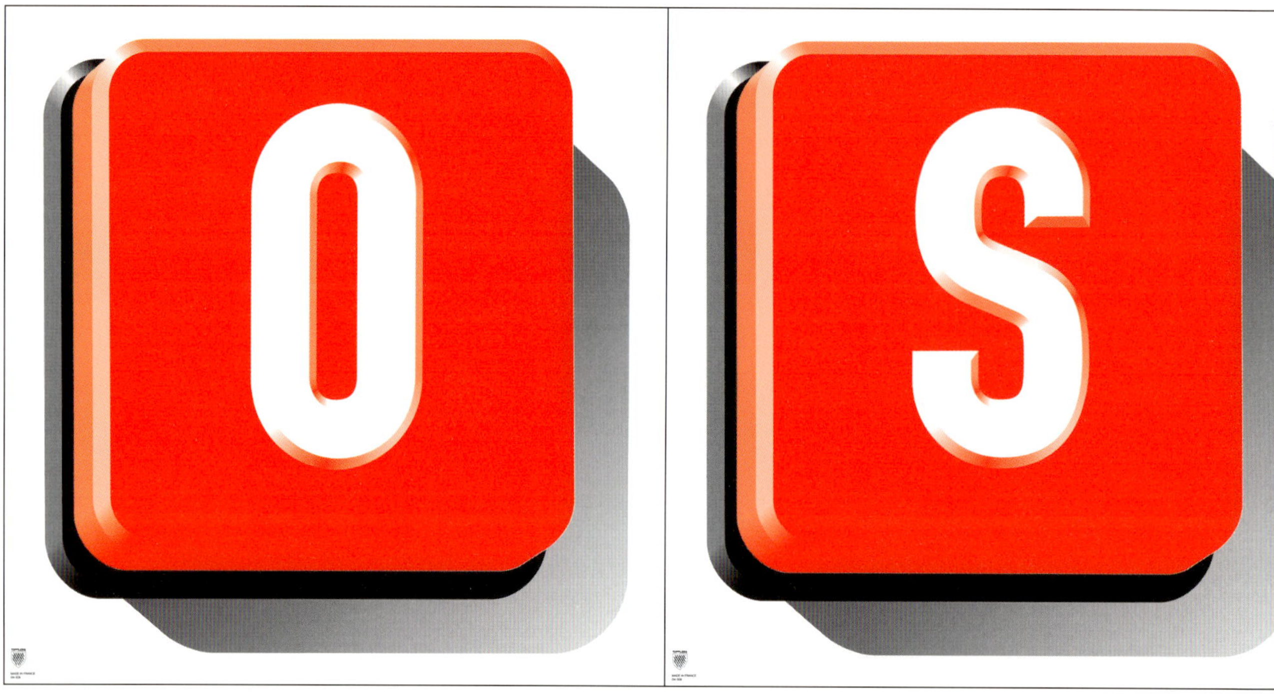
O
S

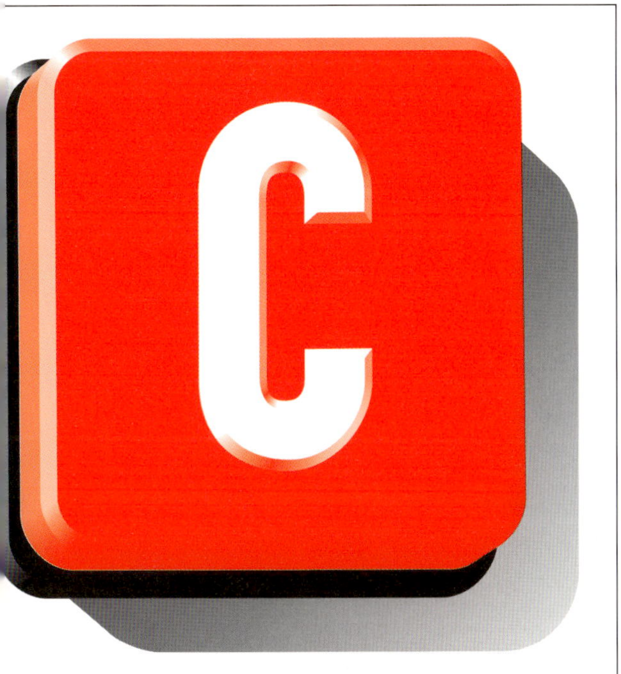

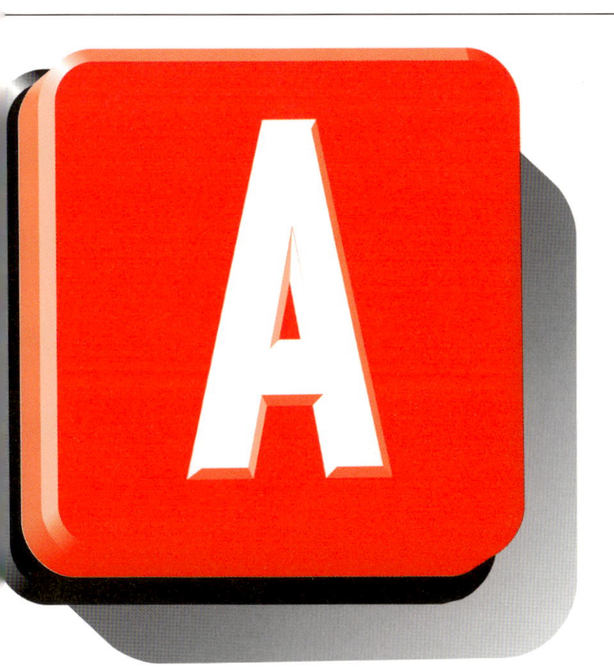

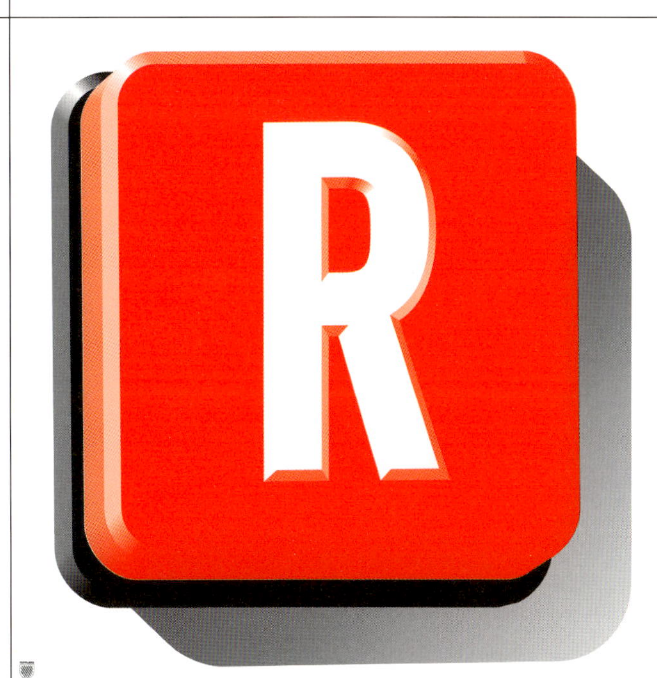

Top Left)	OSCAR / SERGENT BOSSA. EP	2002	DENOTE RECORDS Ltd
Top Middle)	OSCAR / BIG APPLE. EP	2002	DENOTE RECORDS Ltd
Top Right)	OSCAR / PARISIAN SOUL (Ian Pooley Mix). EP	2002	DENOTE RECORDS Ltd
Bottom Left)	OSCAR / A NICE FUSION (Front). EP	2002	DENOTE RECORDS Ltd
Bottom Right)	OSCAR / BRASIL 2030. EP	2002	DENOTE RECORDS Ltd

MISTER J / LOVE CUTZ. EP 2003 MISSIVE

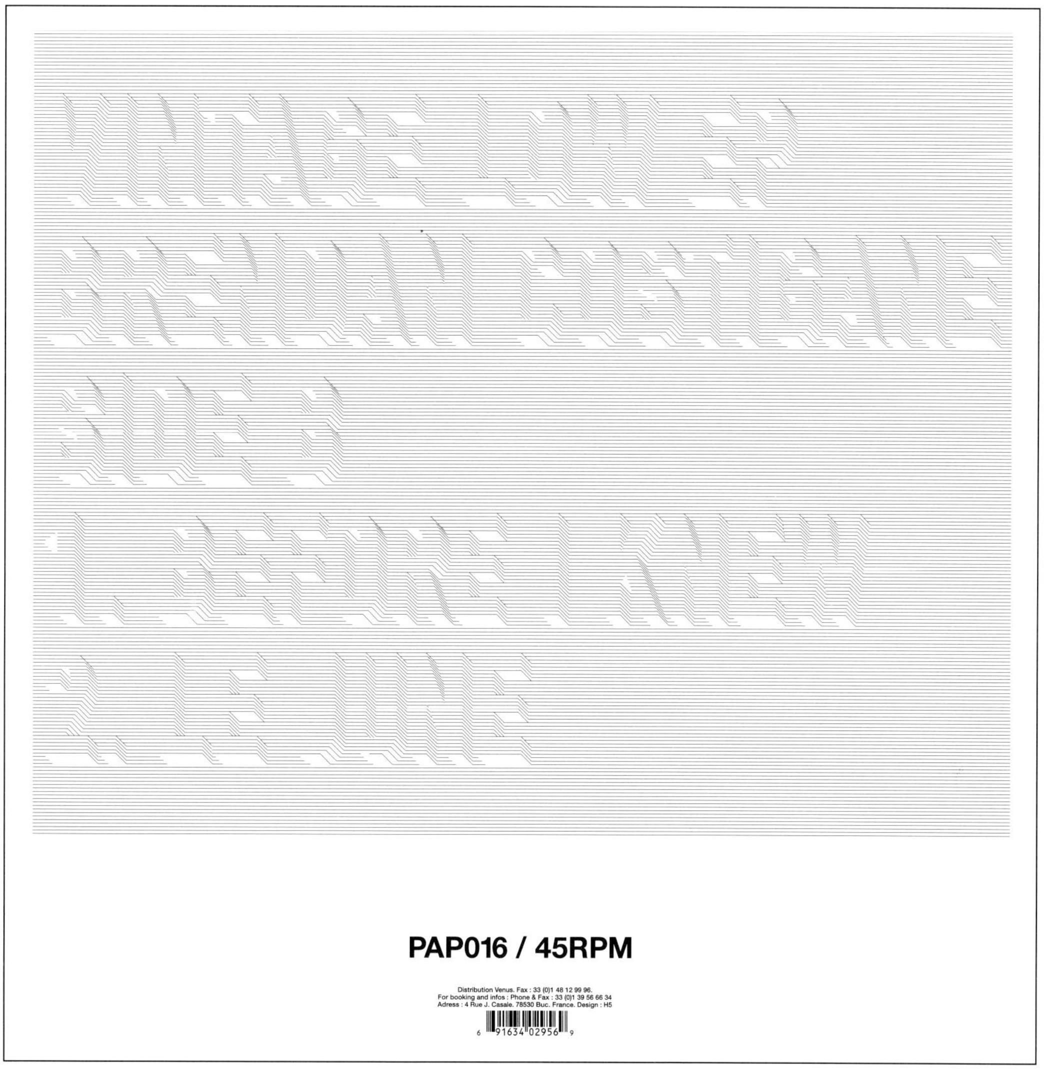

BRENDANE COSTIGANE / VINTAGE LOW. EP 2001 PAMPLEMOUSSE

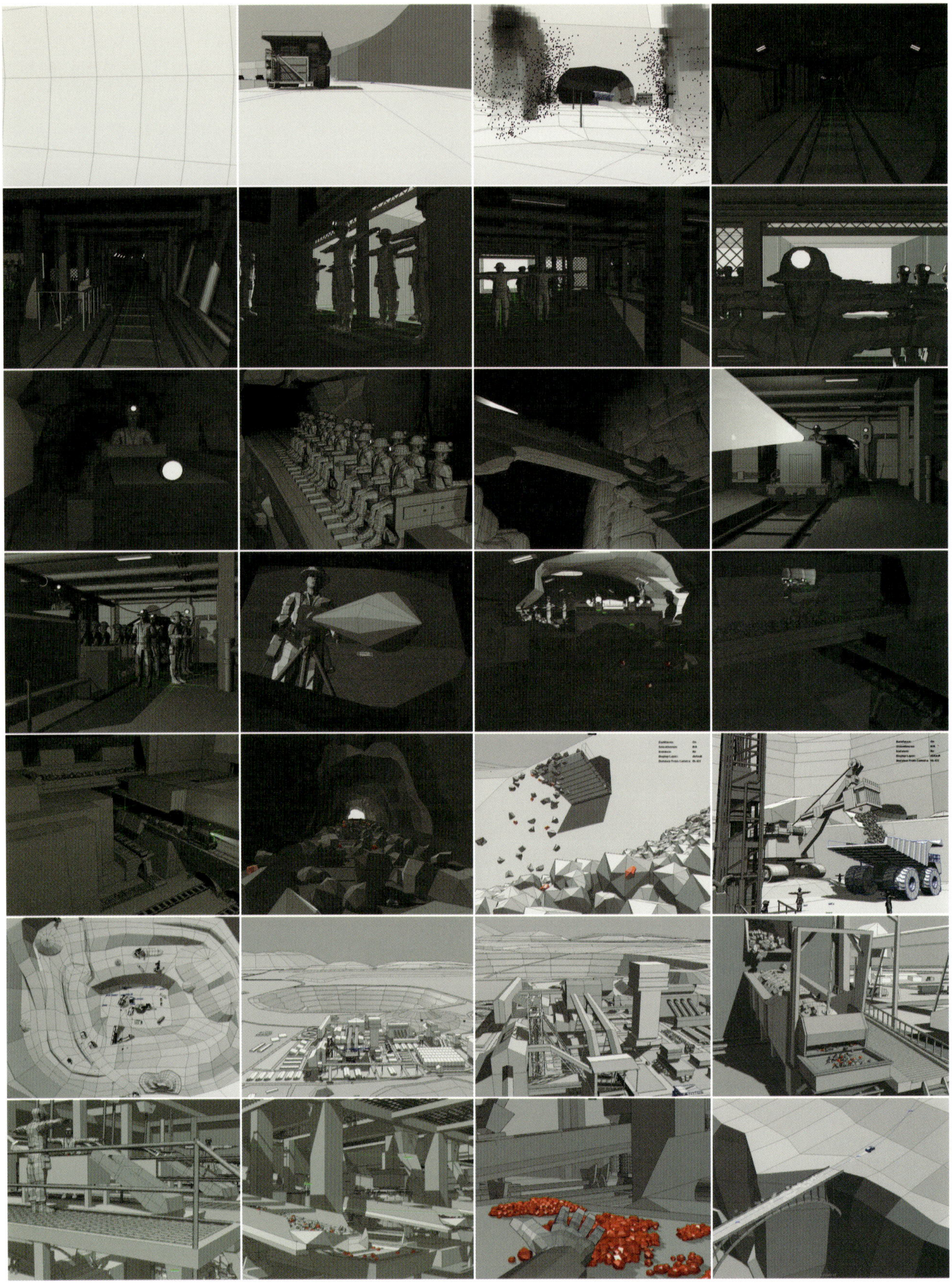

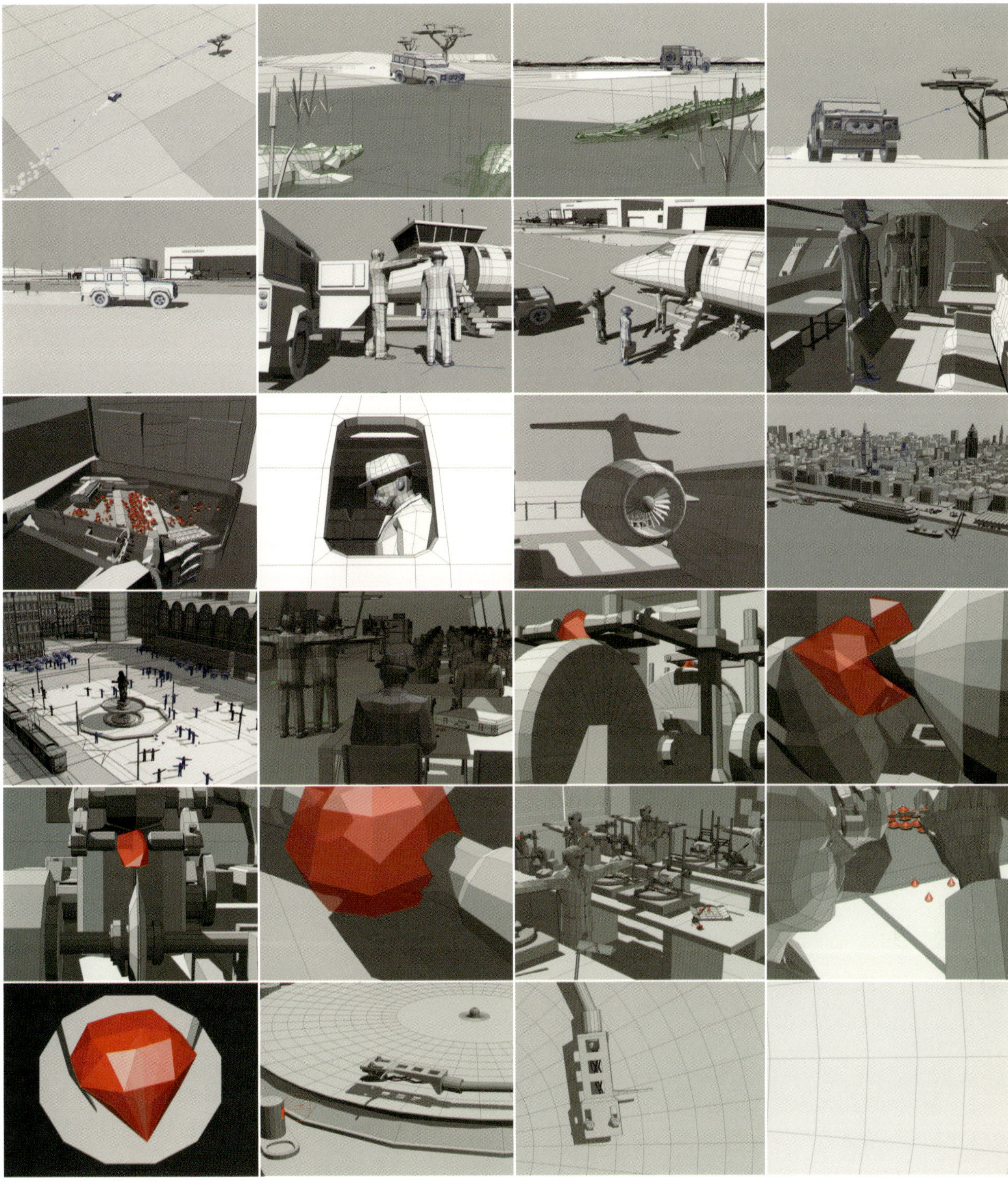

"USE ME" BY WUZ / Video stills from pop-promo

2002

Director: H5
Production: Solid
Post Production: Duran
Labels: V2 / Solid

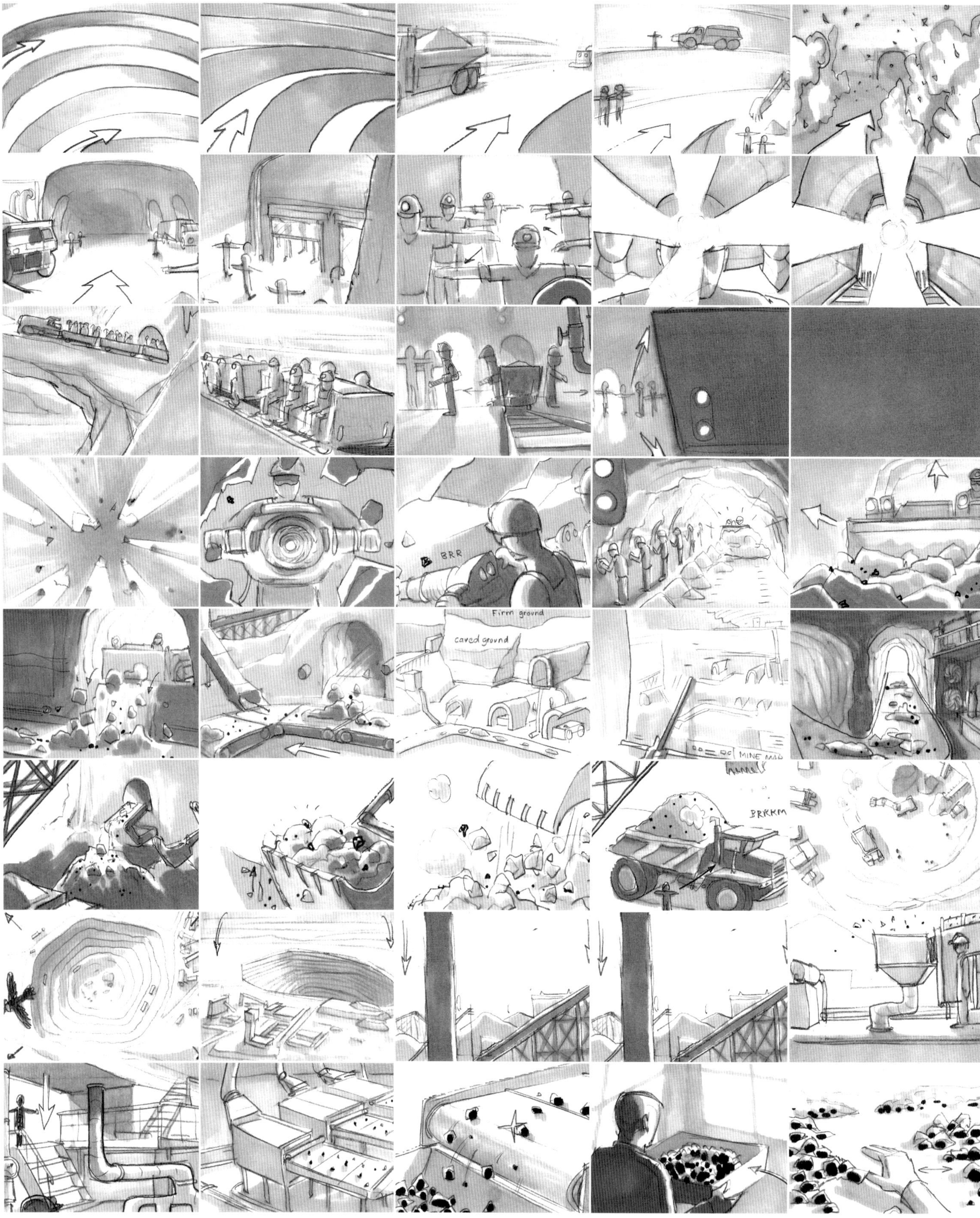
BRR
Firm ground
caved ground
MINE
BRKKM

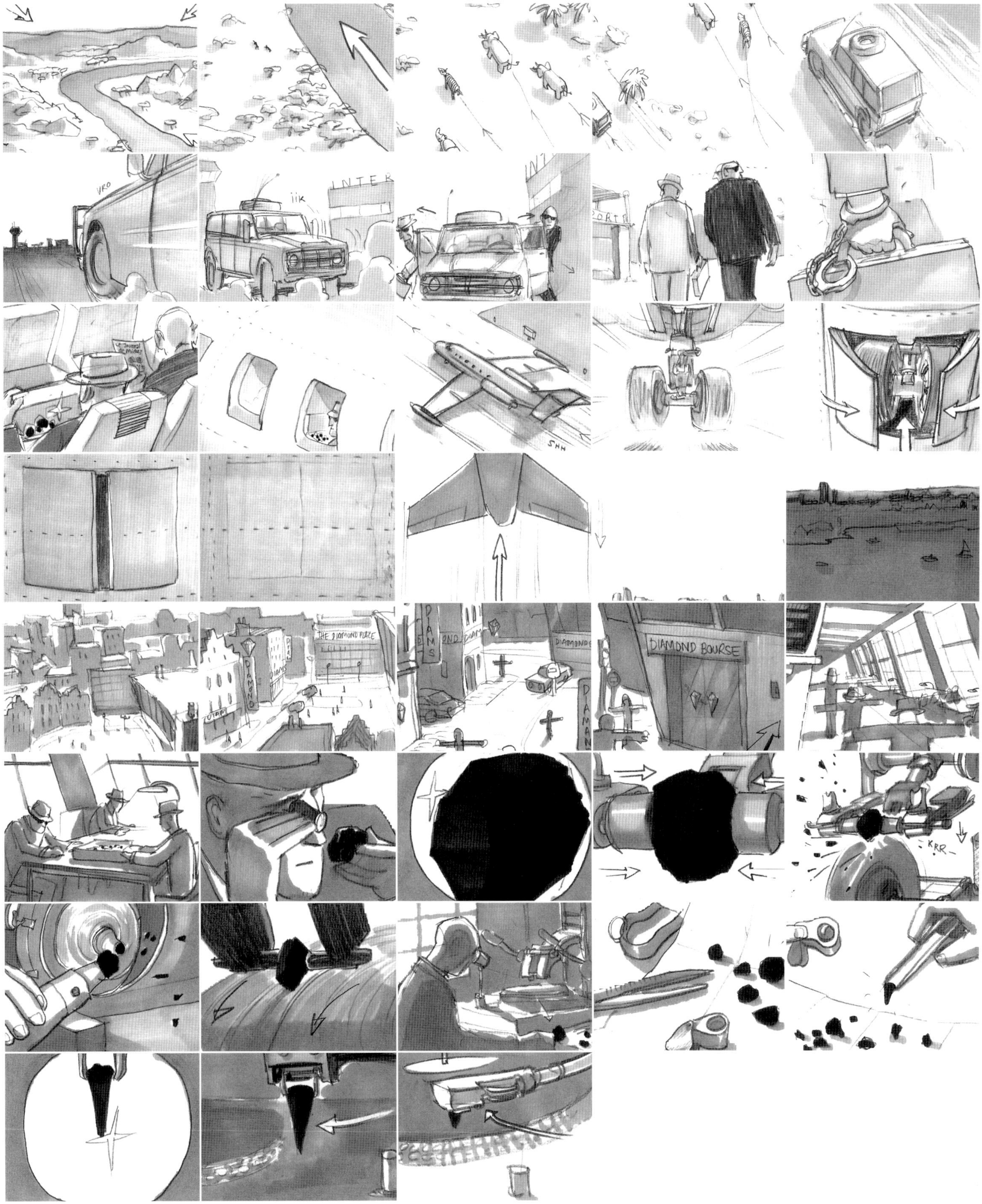

"USE ME" BY WUZ / Story Board

2002

Director: H5
Production: Solid
Post Production: Duran
Labels: V2 / Solid

CHAPTER 03
WHY THE THREAD?

なぜ糸なのか

答え: 理論的には、イメージを作り出す糸の縫い目は見えない方が良い。ここではあえてその糸を前方に置いてみた。そして、日頃見なれている我々とオブジェクトとの距離感をいじくってみた。

WHY THE THREAD?

ANSWER: Ideally, the “thread” that went into creating an image is invisible. Here, it is placed in the foreground, and plays on the distance we’re used to between ourselves and an object.

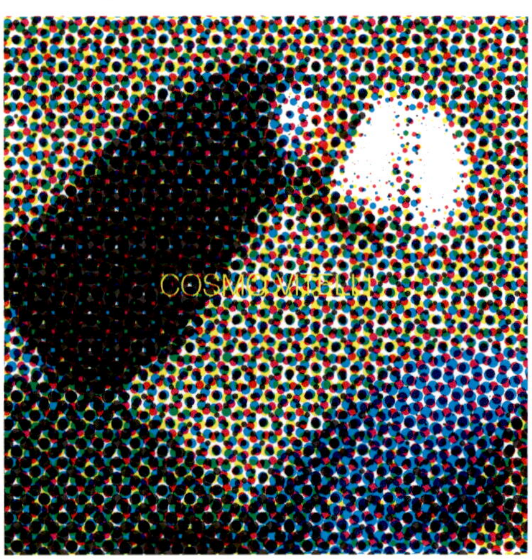

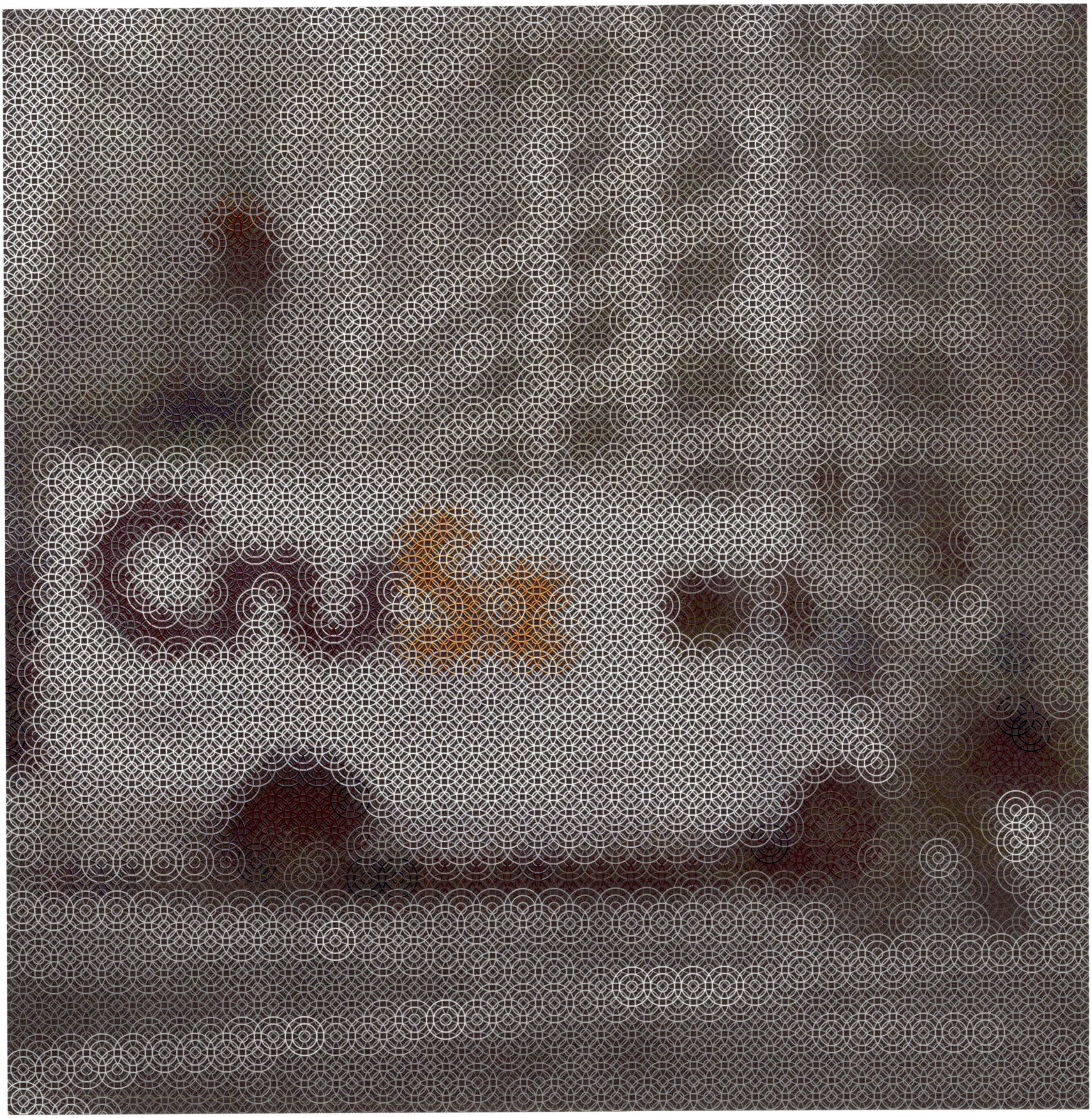

Left Page) COSMO VITELLI / CD Single	1999	V2 / DISQUES SOLID
Right Page) CRUSZ / THERE HAS BEEN A LOT OF WHISPERING ABOUT HIM.... EP	2001	20000ST

CHAPTER 04
WHY IMPULSES?

なぜ衝動的なのか

答え: その時々の衝動をどうやって説明するの？

WHY IMPULSES?

ANSWER: How do you expect us to explain impulses?

Top Left)	BEBOB DAWG / RUMBLE IN RIO. EP	2002	MISSIVE
Top Right)	HENRI GOES DIRTY / NO LIES. EP	2003	PÔLE NORD
Middle Left)	OFFSET. EP	2003	MISSIVE
Middle Right)	DOCTOR OLIVE / THE END OF THE BEGINNING. EP	2004	MISSIVE
Bottom Left)	ELECTRIC KIDS / LIVE TO DANCE. EP	2005	MISSIVE
Bottom Right)	OSCAR / OVERHEAD. EP	1999	DENOTE RECORDS Ltd

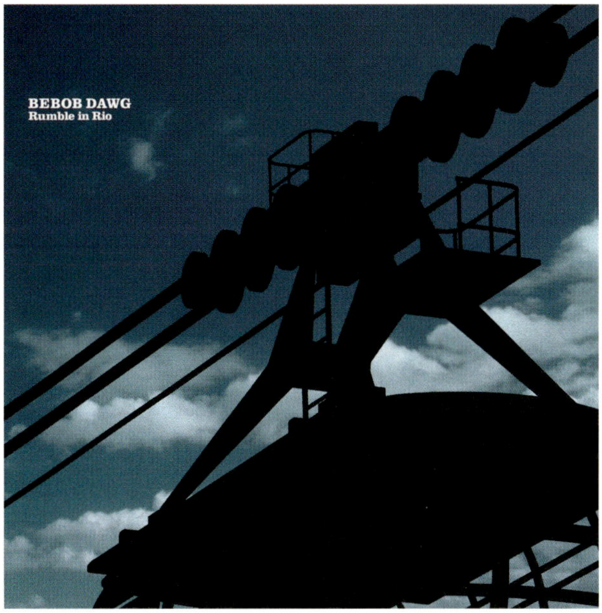
BEBOB DAWG
Rumble in Rio

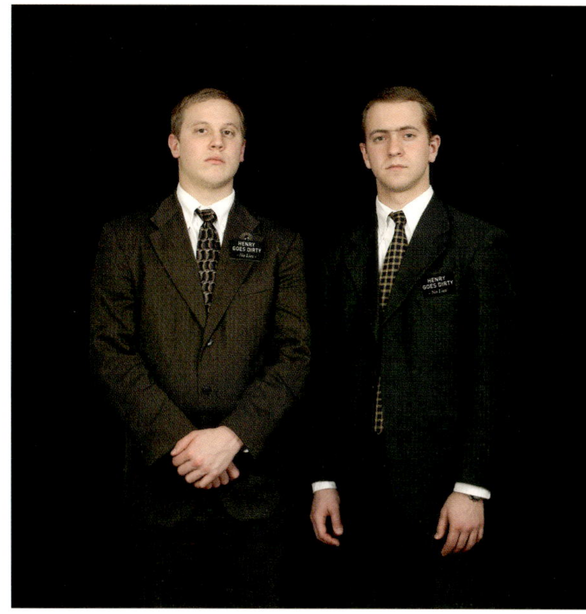
HENRY
GOES DIRTY
HENRY
GOES DIRTY

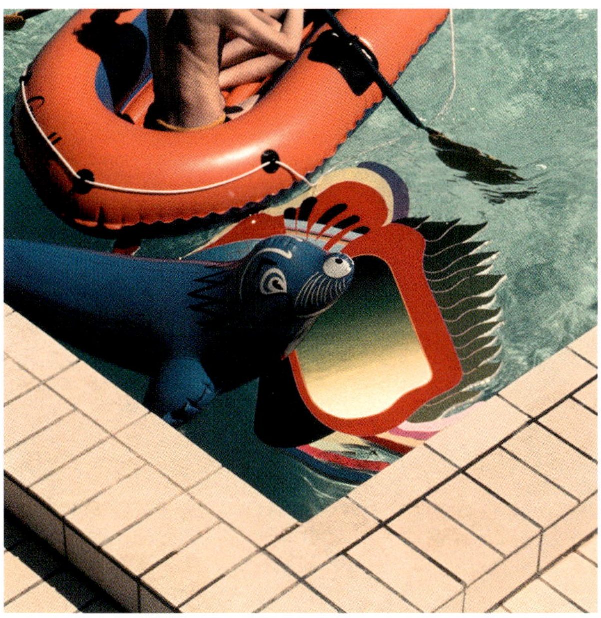

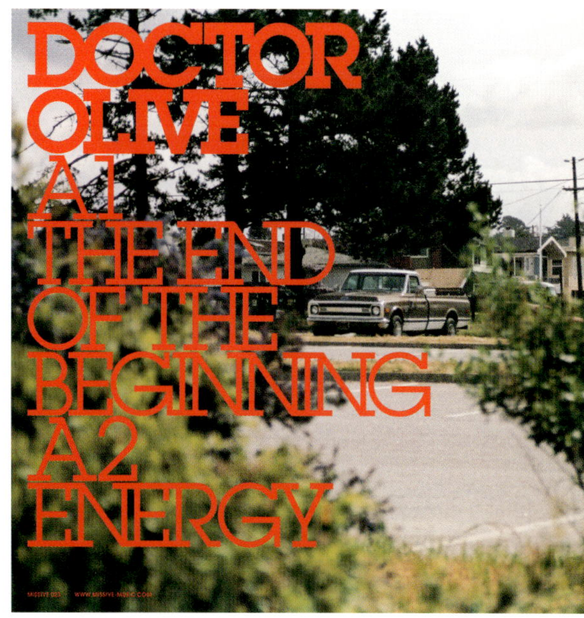
DOCTOR
OLIVE
A1
THE END
OF THE
BEGINNING
A2
ENERGY

6.30 ELECTRIC KIDS LIVE TO DANCE
MISSIVE 26. 3 700077 648262 2004
A1 LIVE TO DANCE AFTER MIX 6.43
PUBLISHED BY MISSIVE MUSIC
WWW.MISSIVE-MUSIC.COM
MADE IN FRANCE

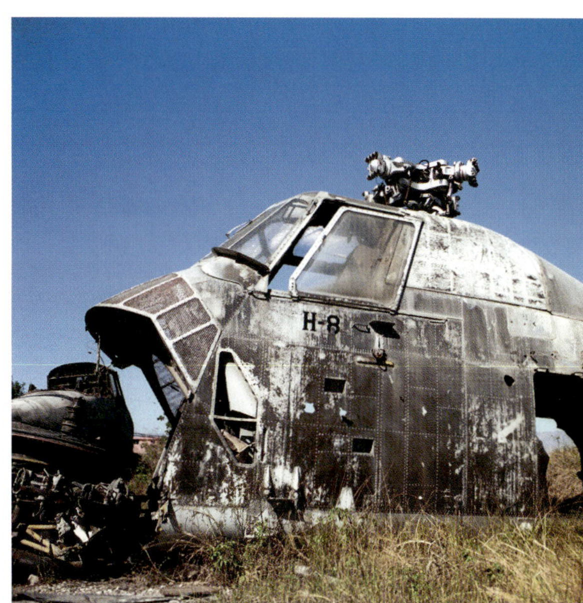
H-8

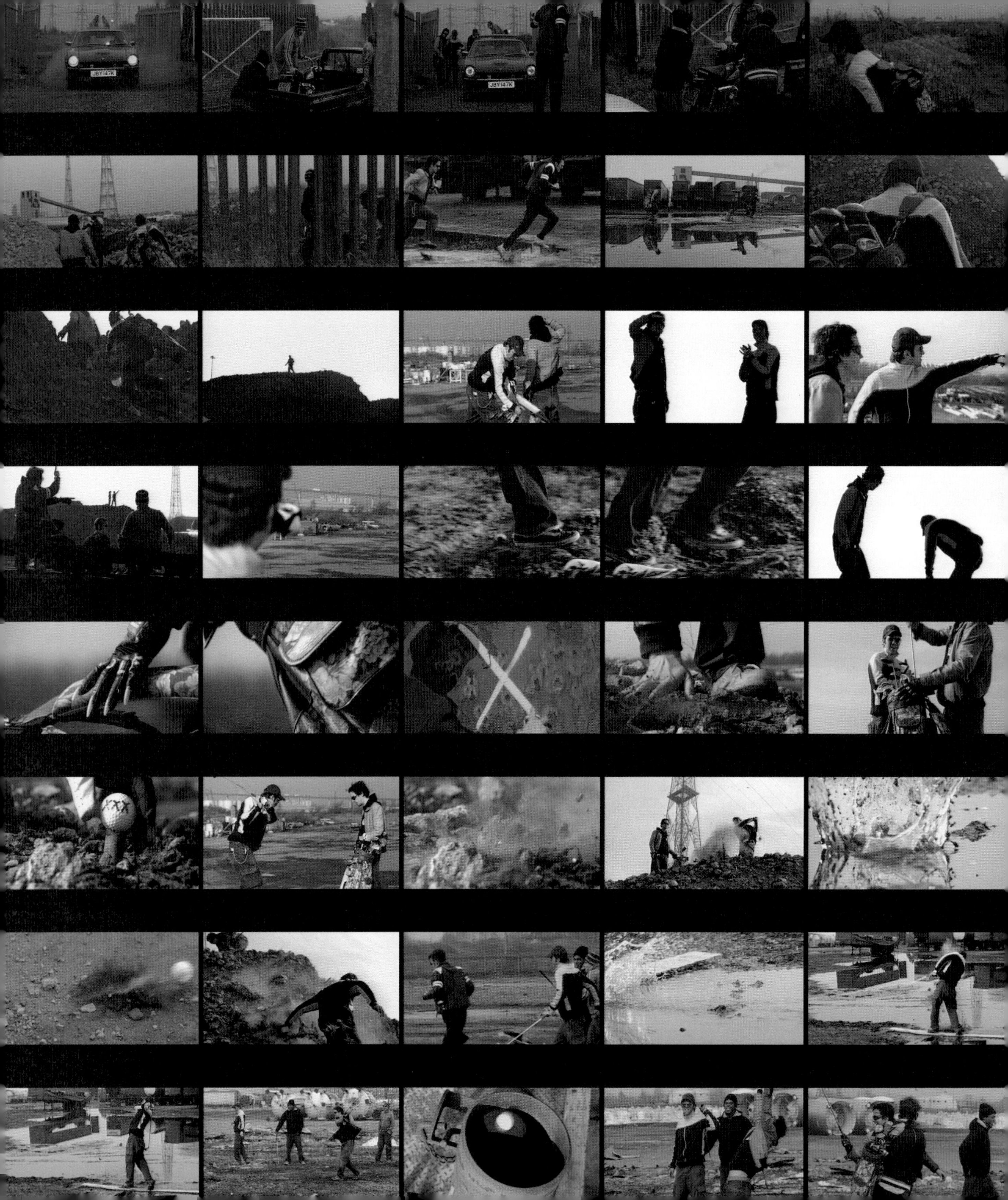
JBY147K
JBY147K

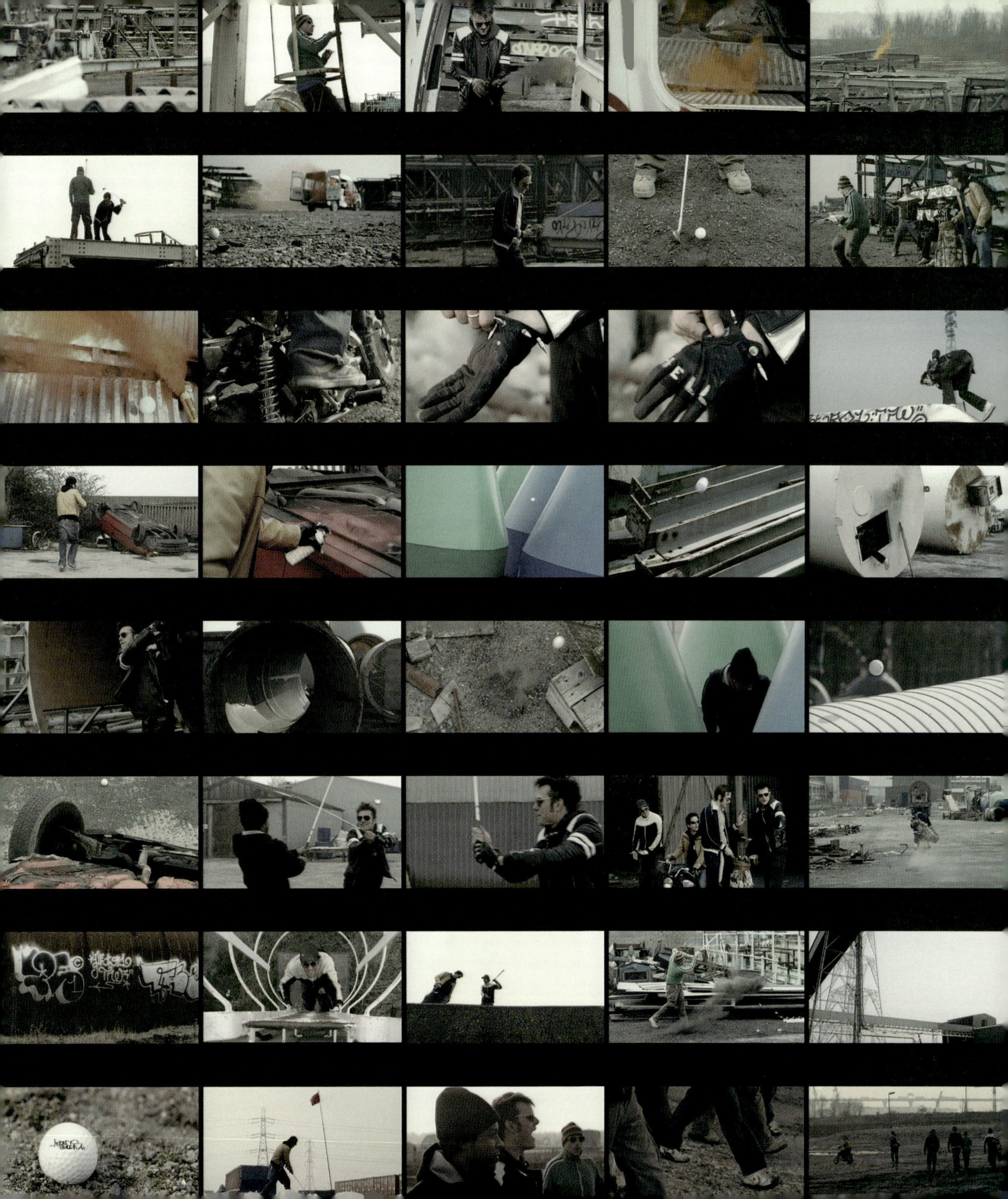

CHAPTER 05 WHY CITIES?

なぜ都市なのか

答え: エレクトロニック音楽の重要な要素である都市。常にインスピレーションの源であり、アレックス・ゴファーの『THE CHILD』やSFA、ルイヴィトンのビデオに見られるように、都市は表現の場となっている。

WHY CITIES?

ANSWER: An integral part of electronic music, the city is naturally a source of inspiration and a space of representation (videos for "The Child", for SFA, for a Louis Vuitton film…).

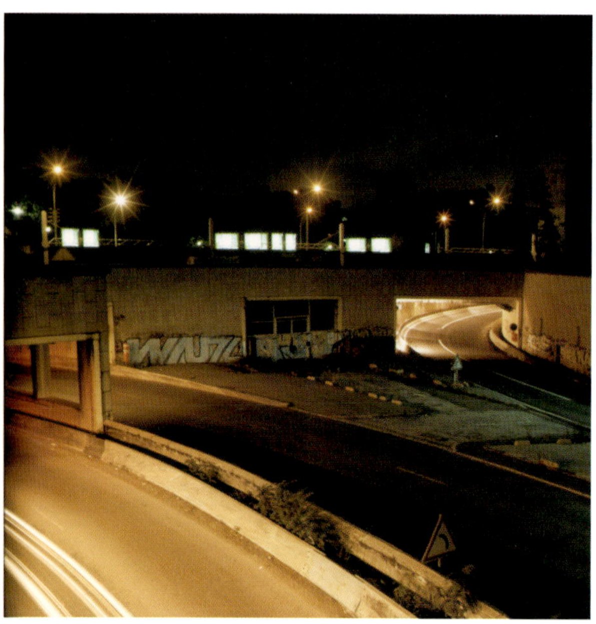

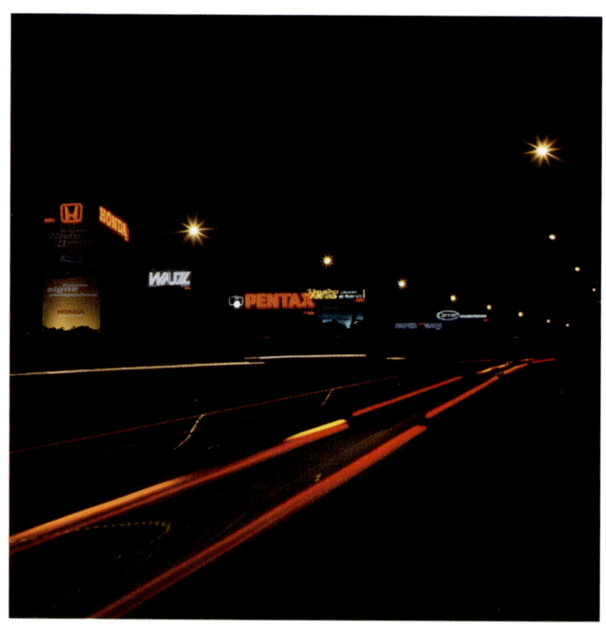

Left Page Left)	WUZ / WITHOUT YOU. CD Single	2002	V2 / DISQUES SOLID
Left Page Right)	WUZ / WUZ. CD Album	2002	V2 / DISQUES SOLID
Right Page)	DEMON / MIDNIGHT FUNK. CD Album	1999	SMALL / 20000ST

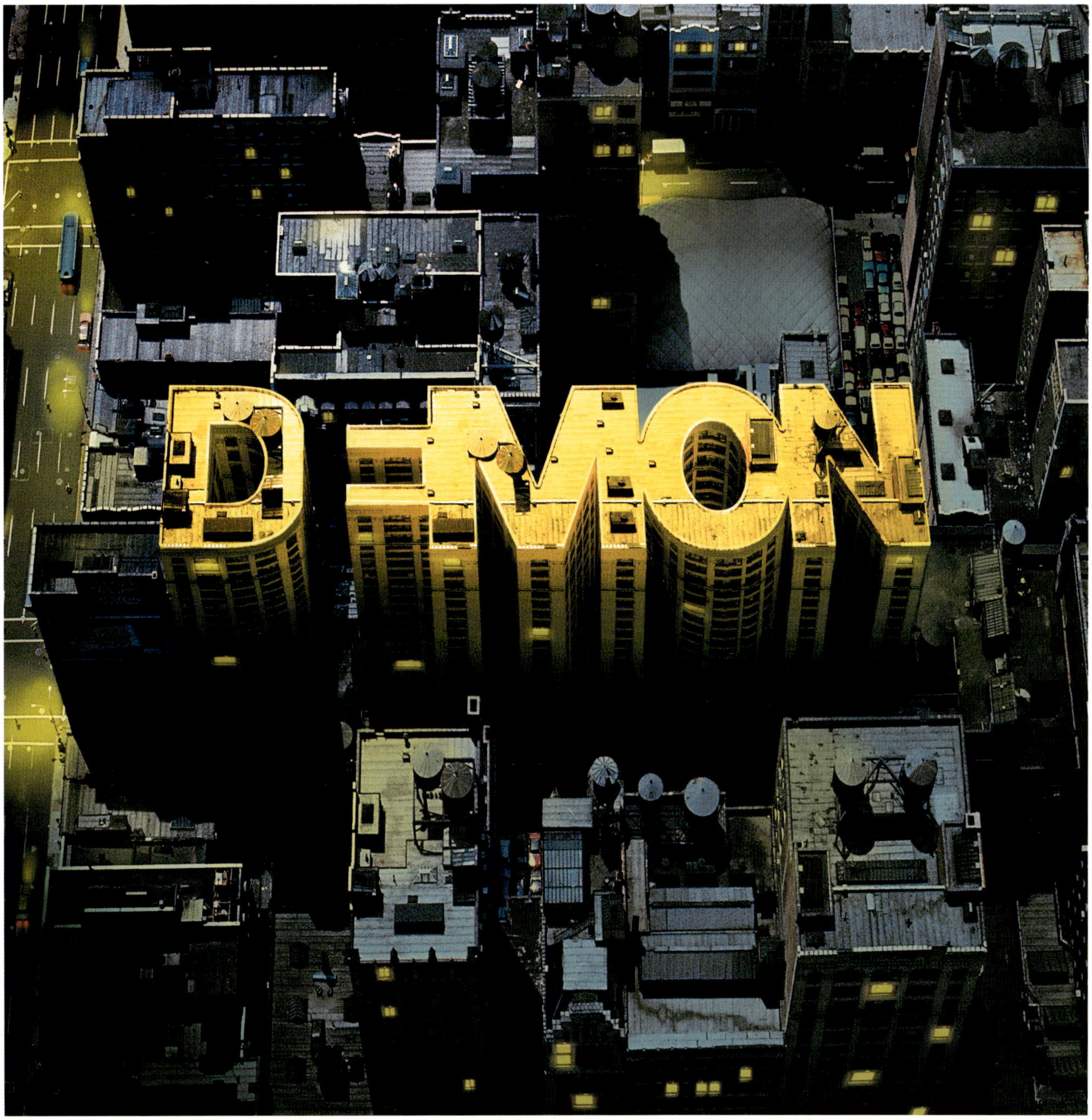
DEMON

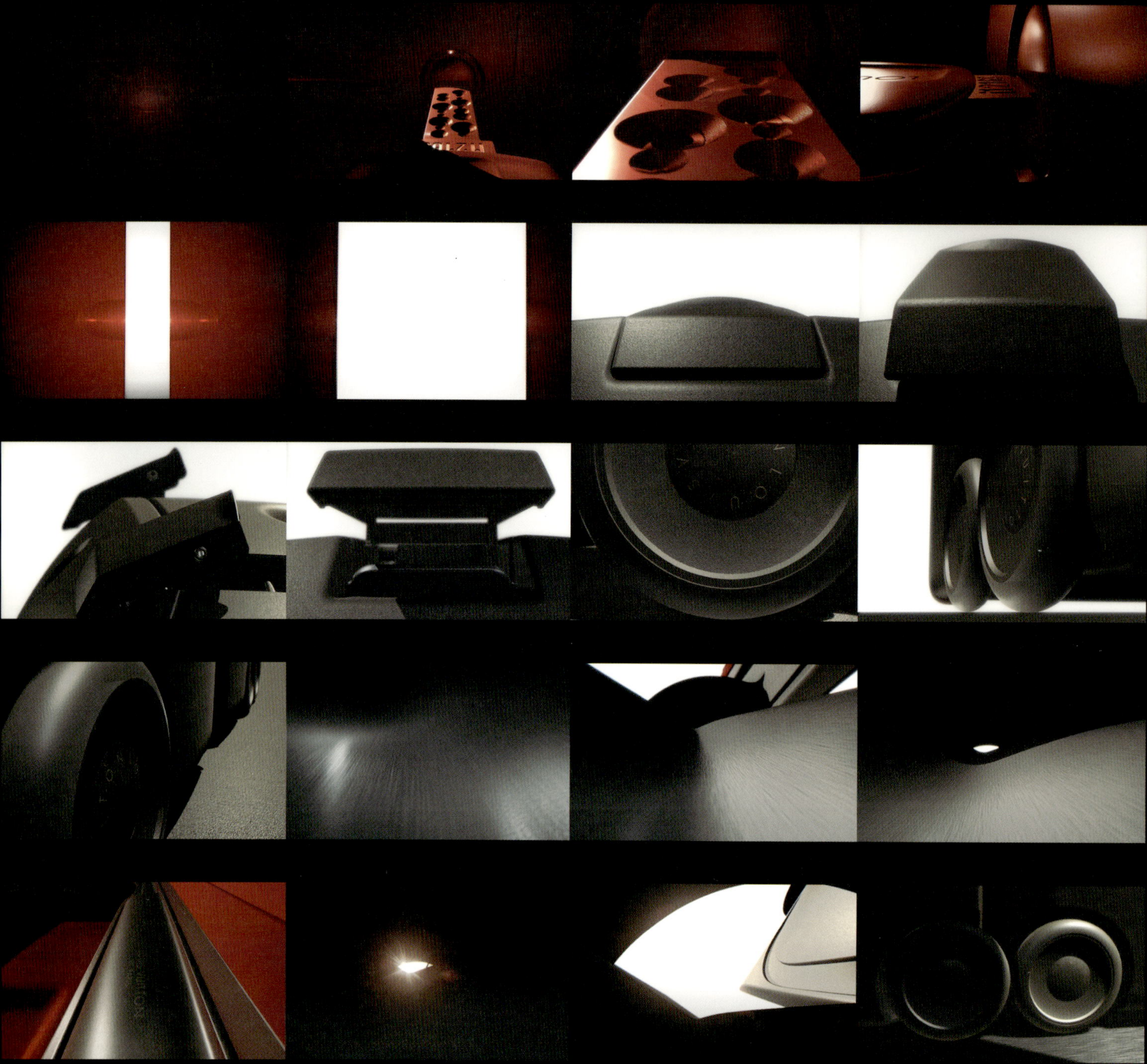

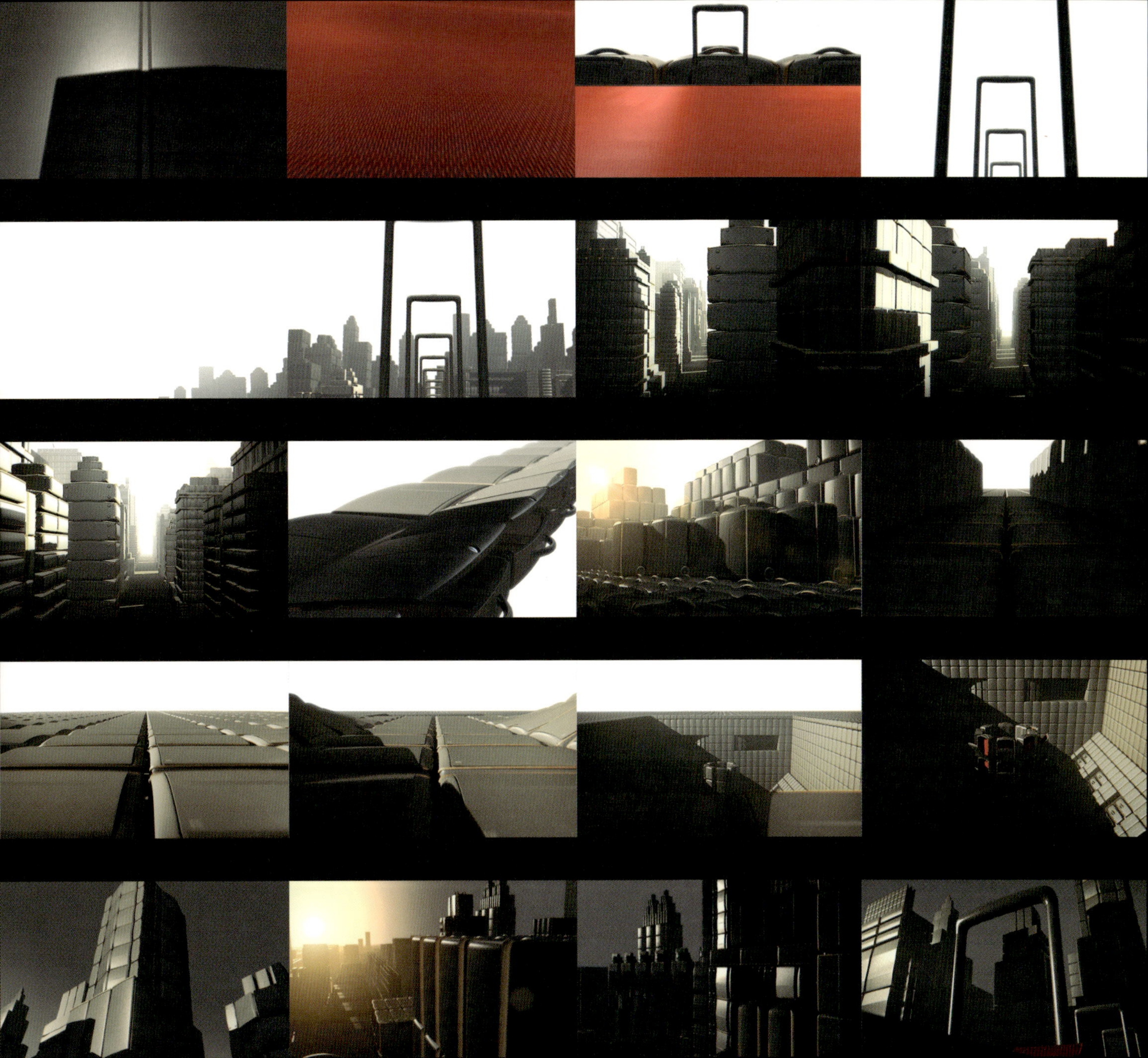

CHAPTER 06
WHY CENSORSHIP?

なぜ検閲なのか

答え: 「どのビデオについても、MTVに対するスクリプトの提出が義務付けられる。あからさまな性や暴力の描写、またはセックス、暴力、ロゴを暗示しているものは、認められない。」*レコード会社の規定により。*

WHY CENSORSHIP?

ANSWER: "For each video, we have to submit a script to MTV, which doesn't tolerate an explicit vision/representation of sex, weapons or logos." *Record company brief.*

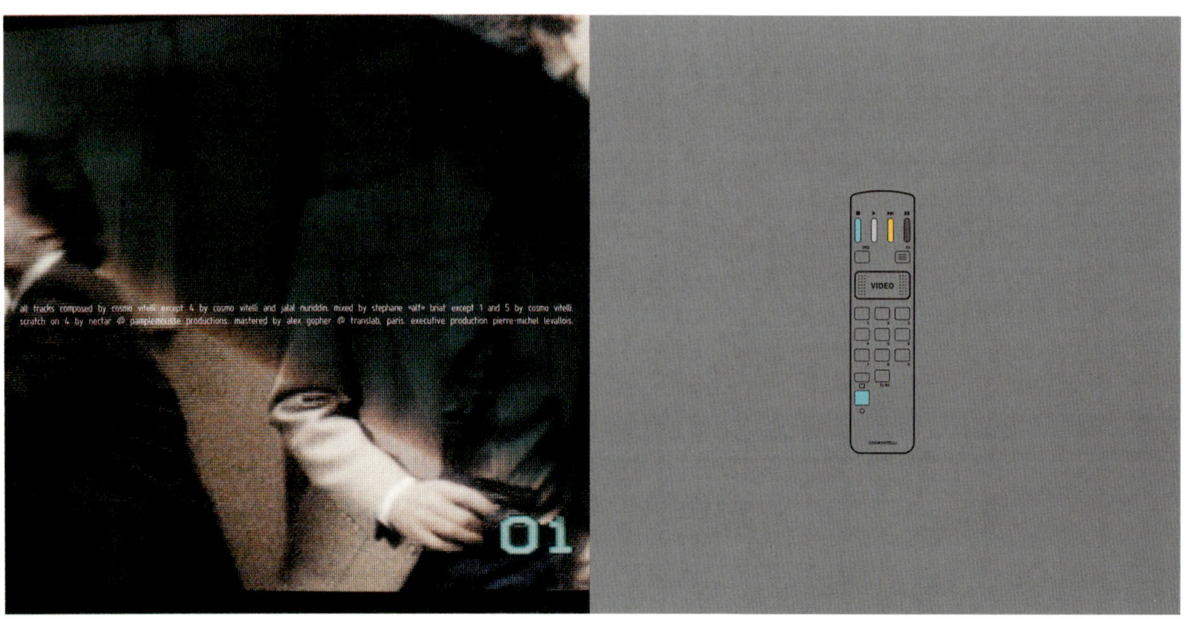

COSMO VITELLI / VIDEO. CD Album (Inner Gatefold) 1998 V2 / DISQUES SOLID

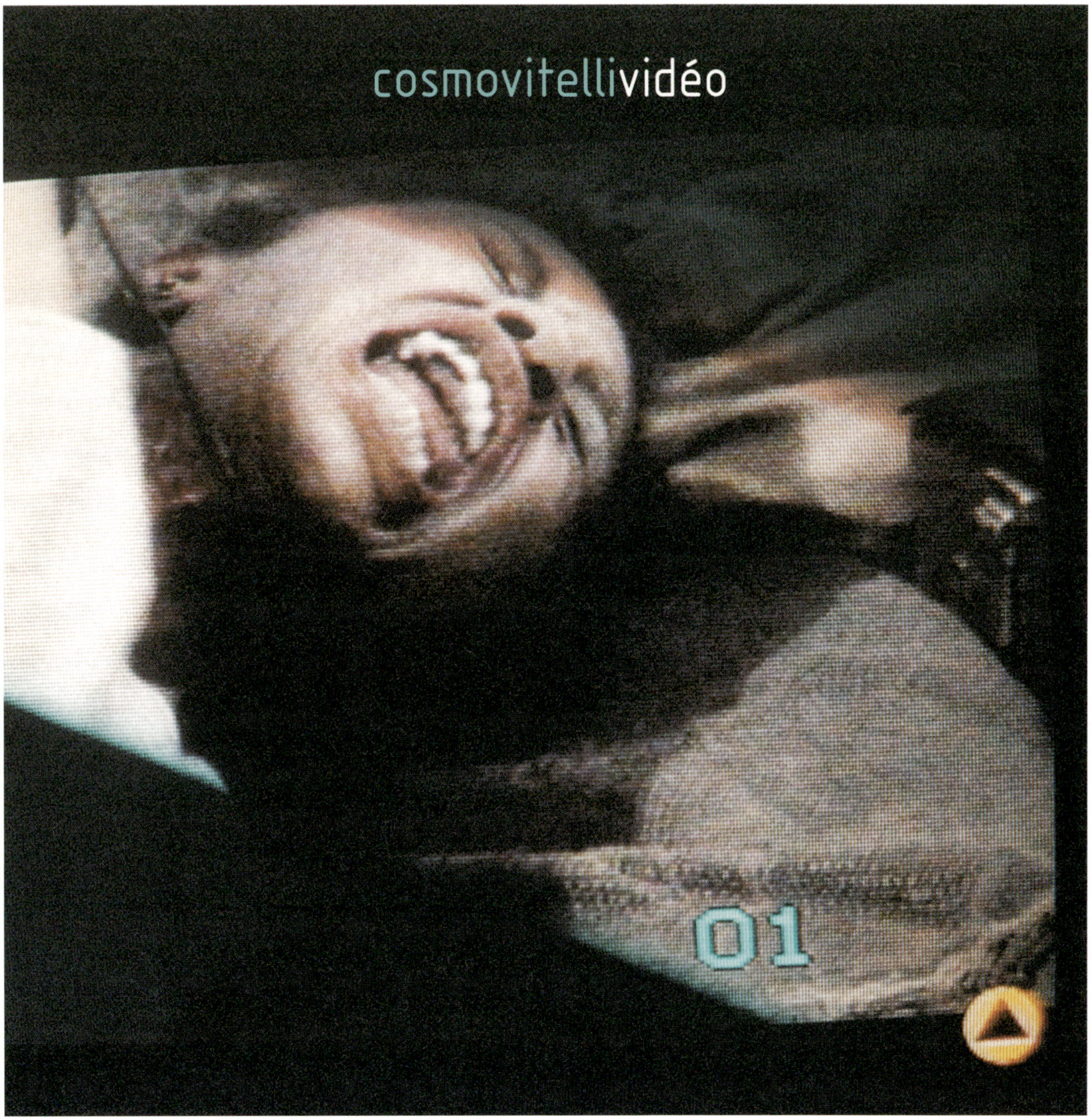

COSMO VITELLI / VIDEO. CD Album (Front) 1998 V2 / DISQUES SOLID

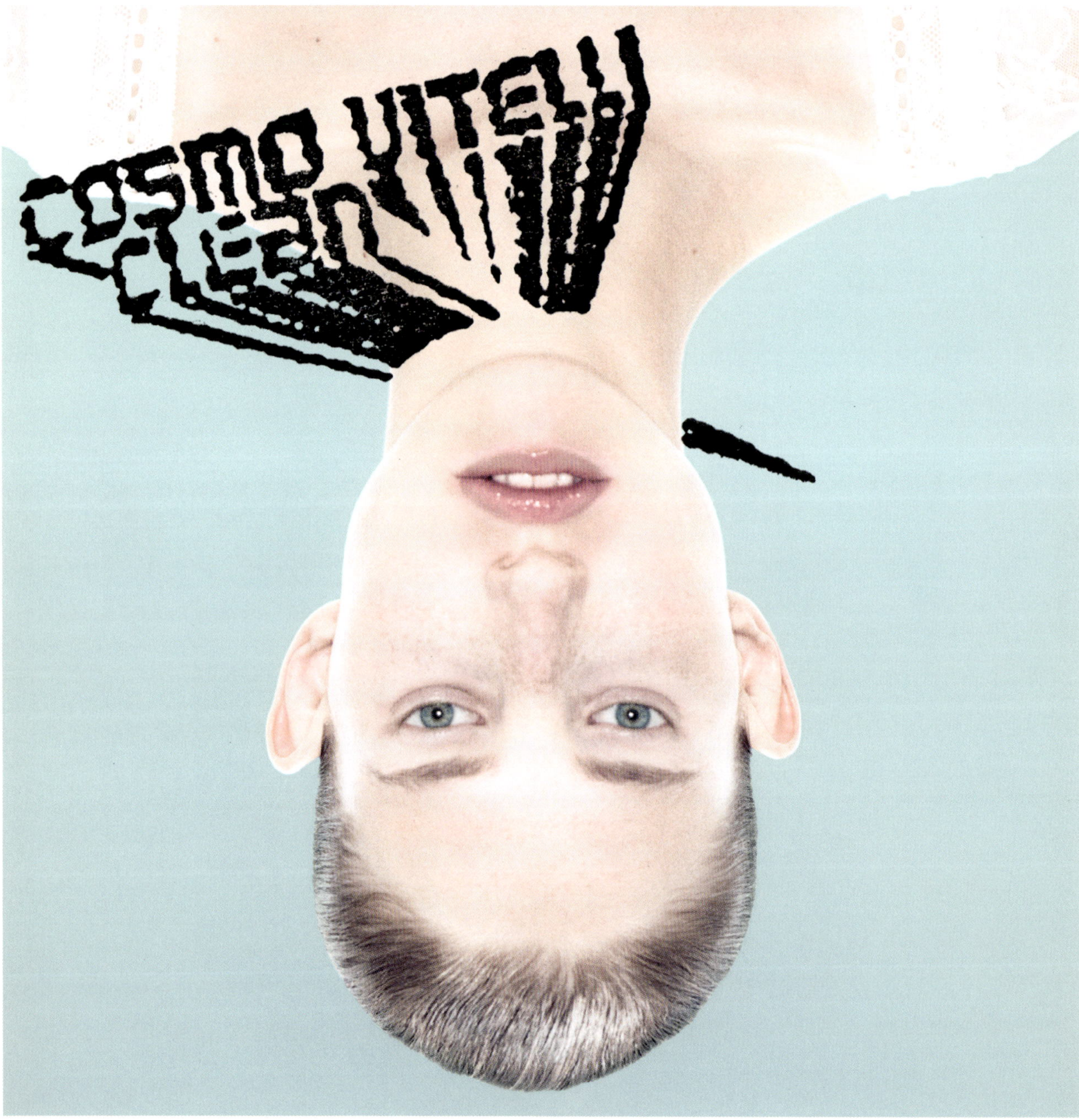

COSMO VITELLI / CLEAN. CD ALBUM (FRONT) 2003 Labels / DISQUES SOLID

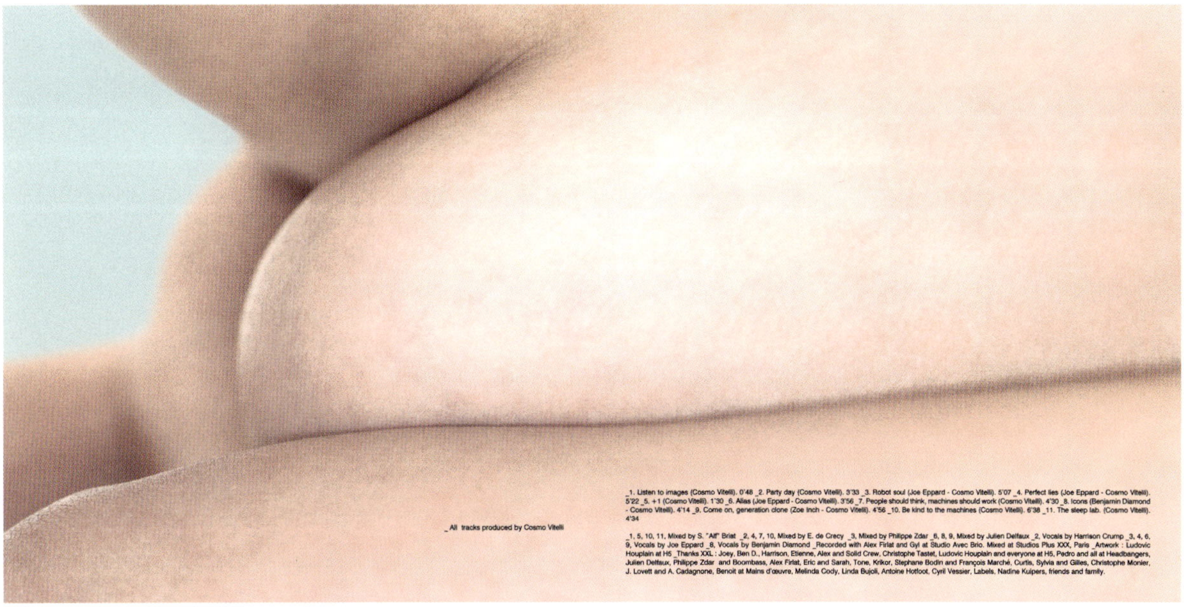

COSMO VITELLI / CLEAN. CD Album (Inner Gatefold) 2003 Labels / DISQUES SOLID

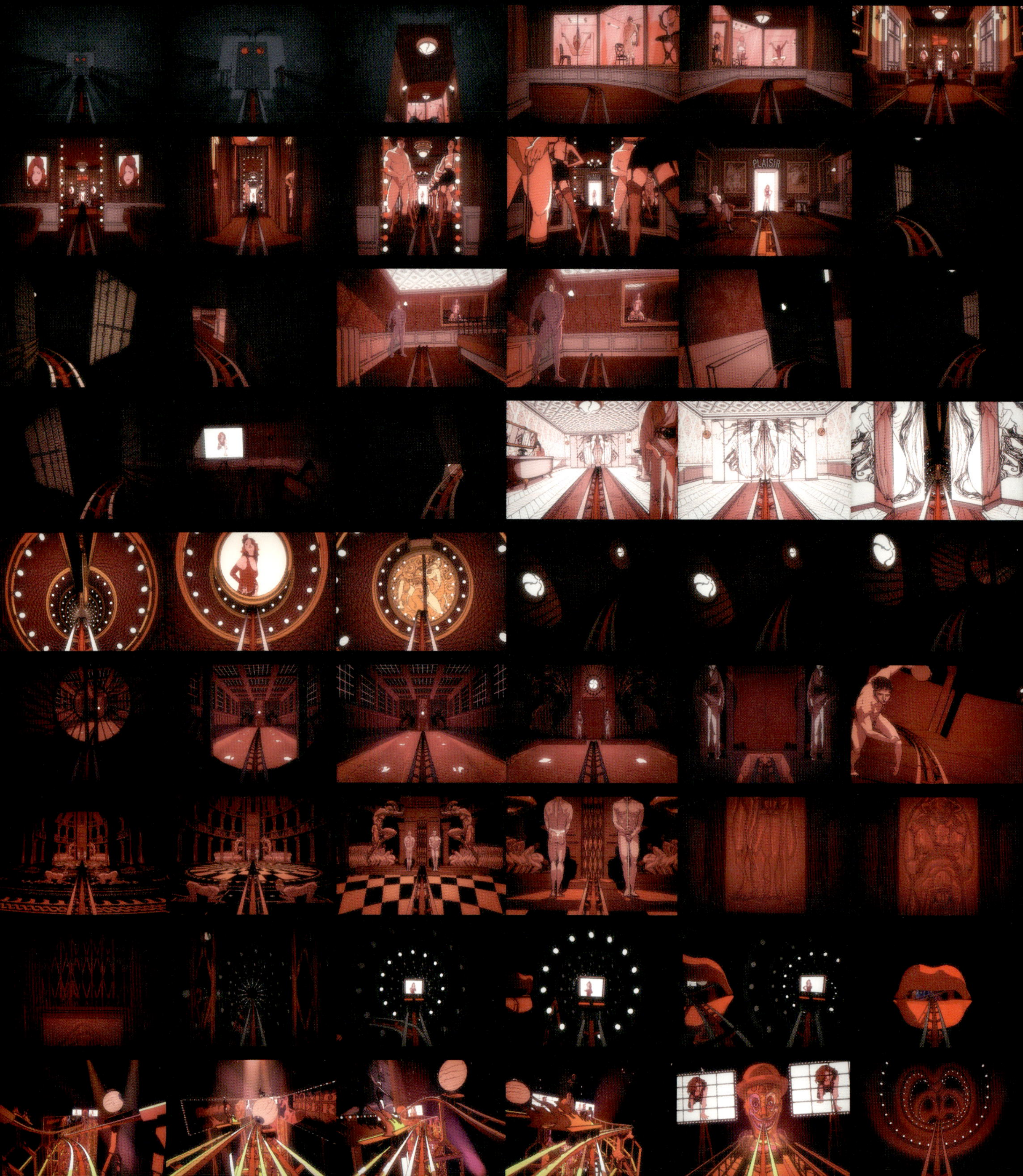
PLAISIR

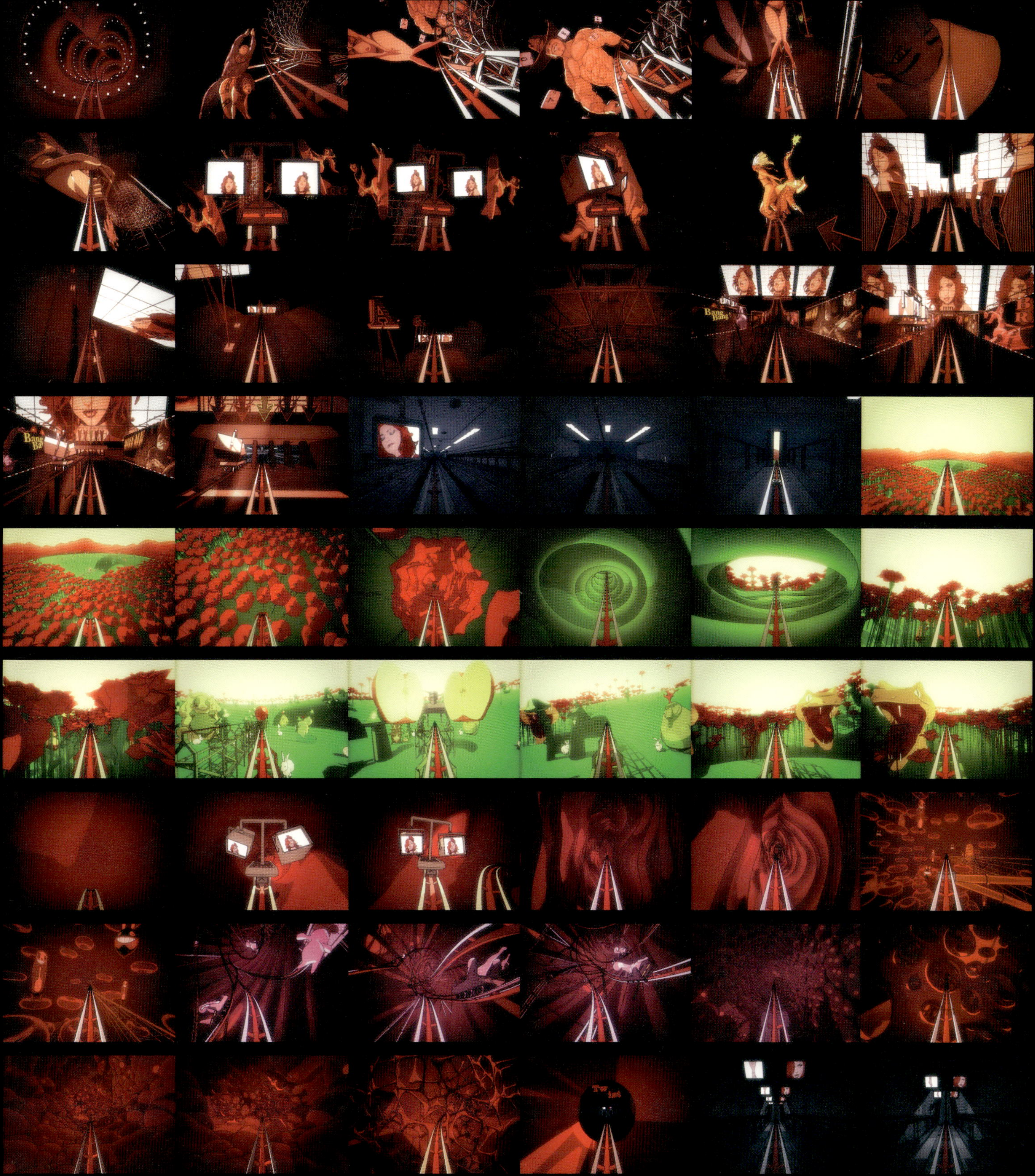

"TWIST" BY GOLDFRAPP / Video stills from pop-promo

2003

Director: H5
Production: Black Dog Films
Post Production: The Mill
Labels: Mute UK

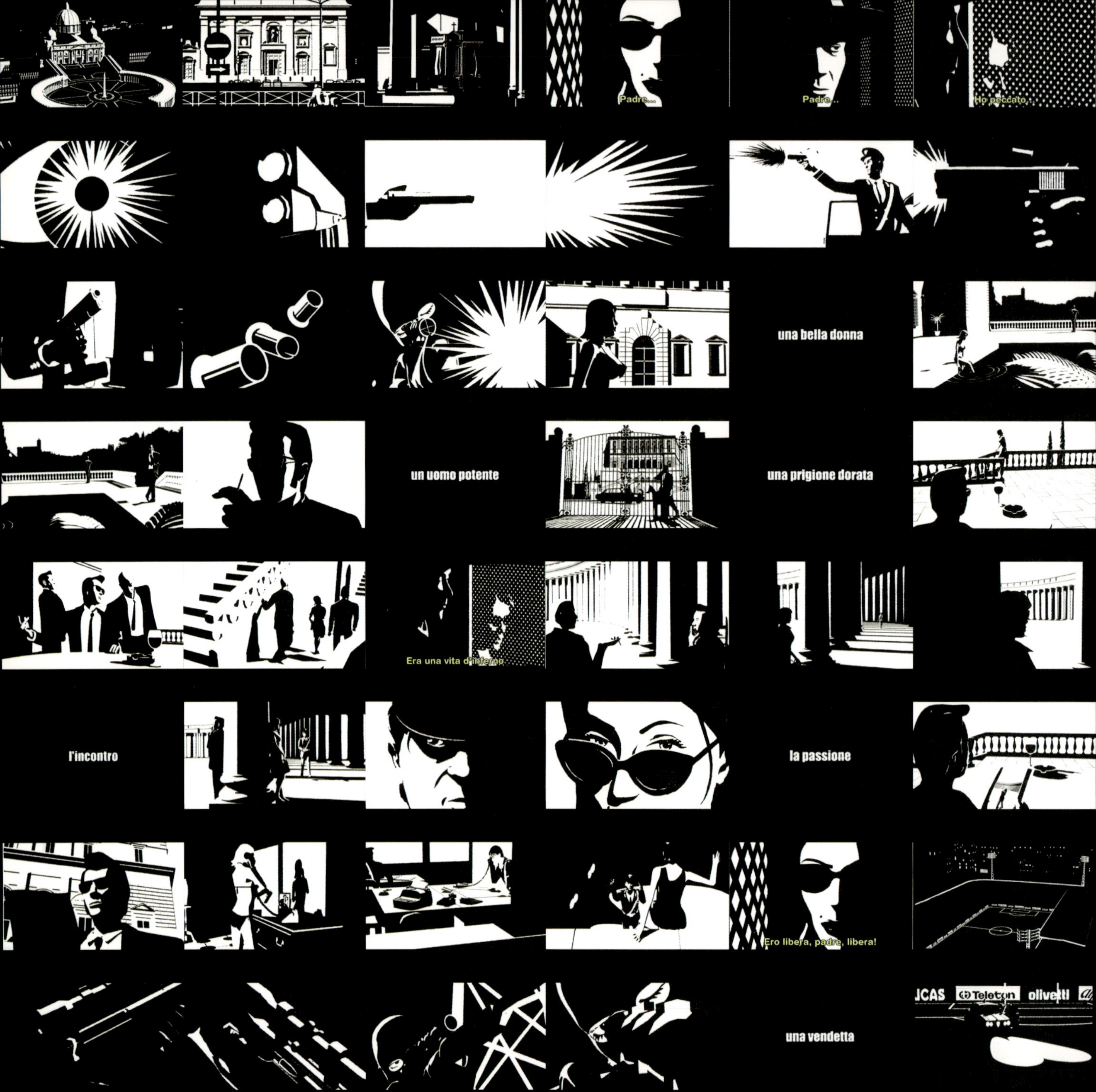
Padre...
Padre...
Ho peccato...
una bella donna
un uomo potente
una prigione dorata
Era una vita d'inferno
l'incontro
la passione
Ero libera, padre, libera!
una vendetta
Teleton
olivetti

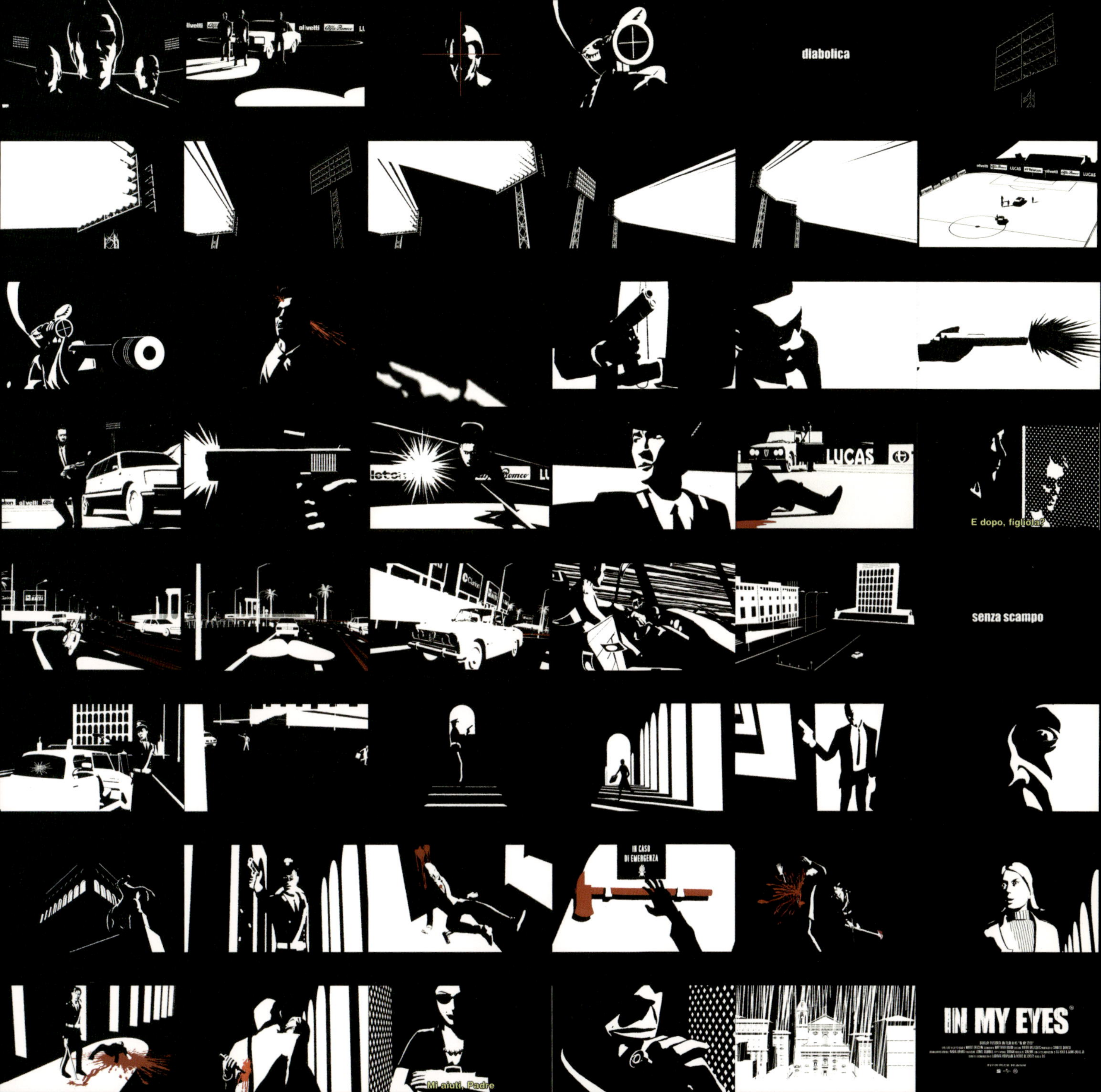

olivetti
diabolica
olivetti
LUCAS
LUCAS
E dopo, figliola?
senza scampo
IN CASO
DI EMERGENZA
Mi aiuti, Padre
IN MY EYES

CHAPTER 07
WHY MINIMALISM?

なぜミニマリズムなのか

答え: ミニマリズムは、単純なものとは違う。ミニマリズムには純粋なものが秘められている。装飾的なものは排除され、機能的なビジュアルとグラフィックに置き換えられる。

WHY MINIMALISM?

ANSWER: Minimalism isn't simplicity; it is, on the contrary, about composing something pure, where the decorative gives way to visual and graphic efficiency.

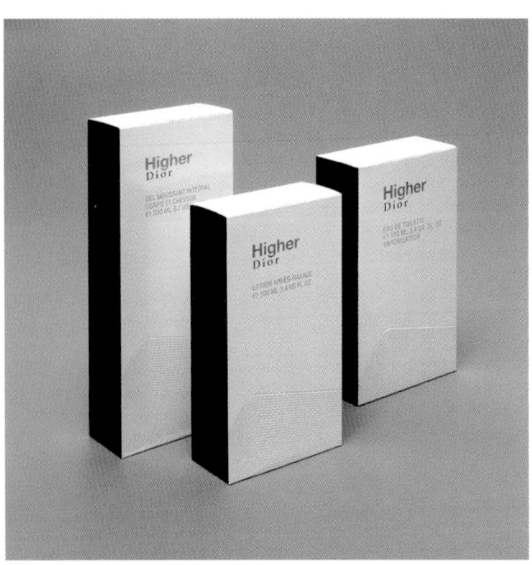

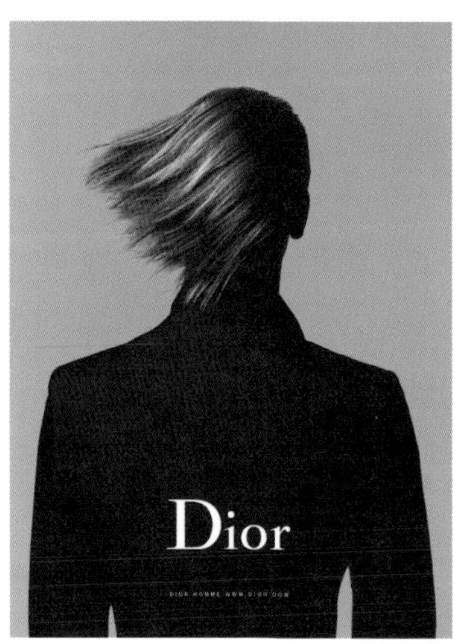

This Page Left) DIOR HIGHER / Packaging 2001
This Page Right) DIOR HOMME / Advertising 2001
Right Page) DIOR HIGHER / Packaging Pattern 2001

Photo: Richard Avedon

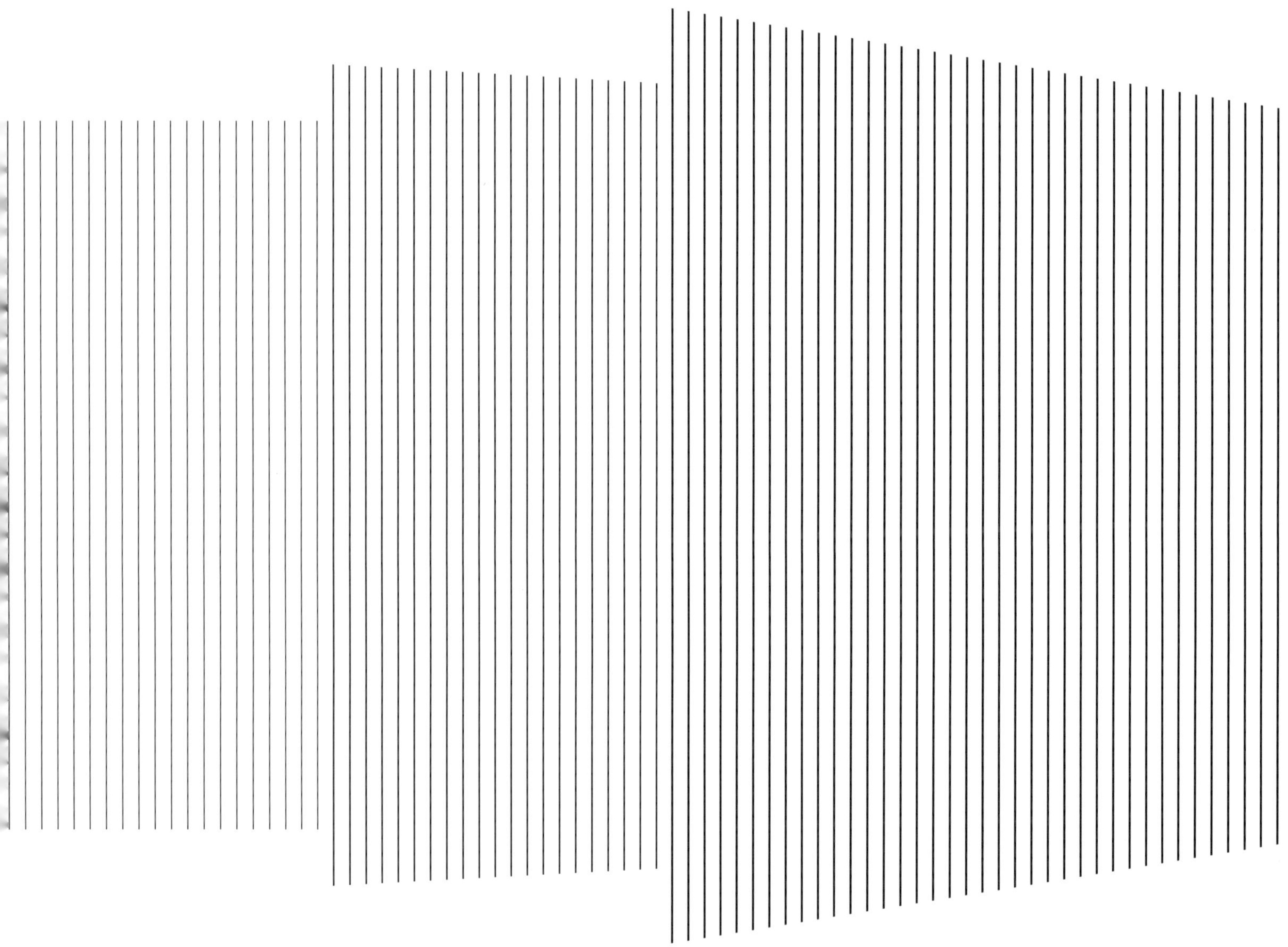

VISIONAIRE / Double Page 2000 H5 for Visionaire / Hedi Slimane

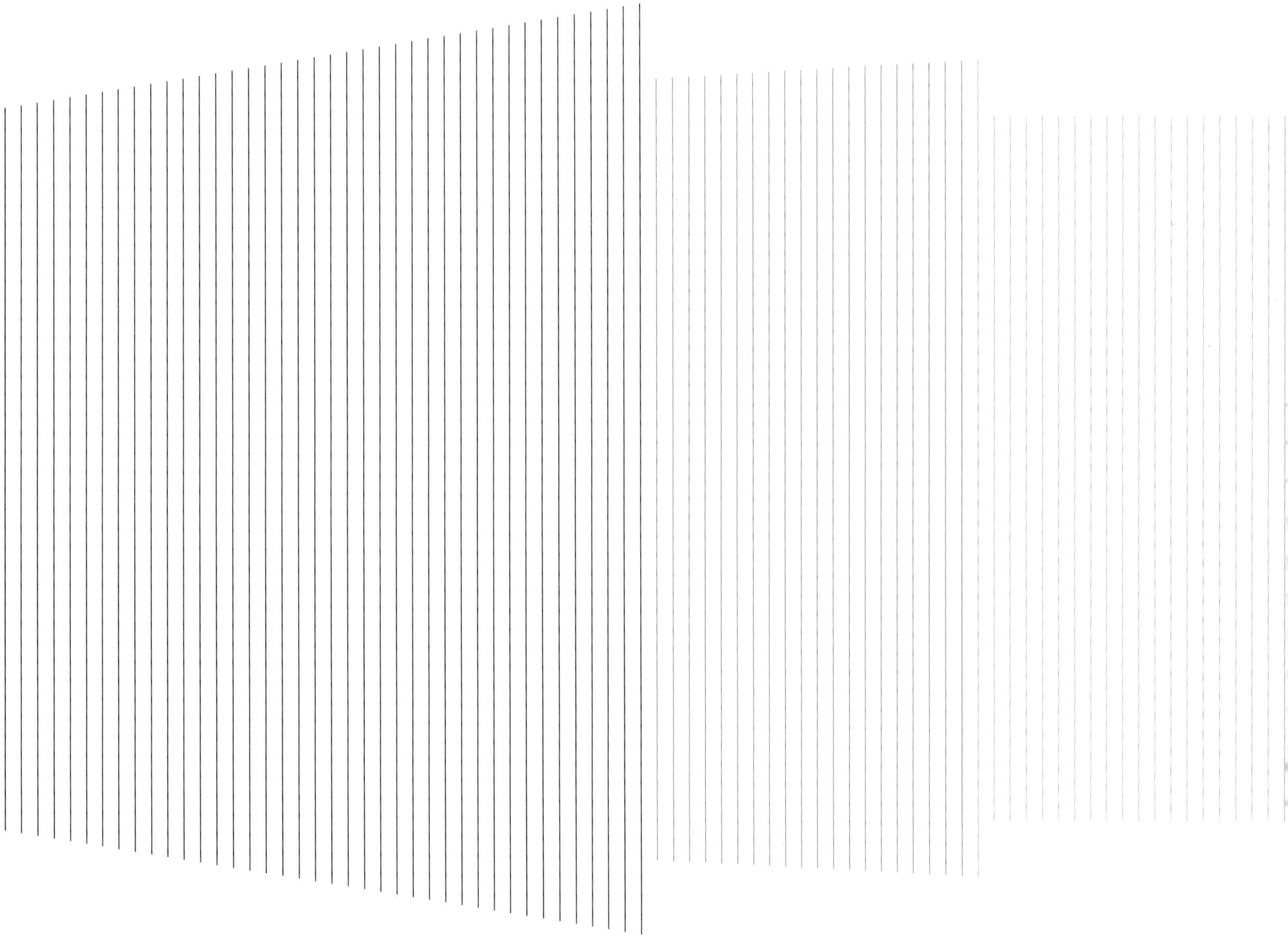

CHAPTER 08 WHY SCHEMATIC?

なぜ図表なのか

答え: ユーザーマニュアルを改造し、その機能性と効率性のみを維持する。そうすることにより、このグラフィック言語は「美」となって生まれ変わる。

WHY SCHEMATIC?

ANSWER: By subverting a user's manual, we keep its functionality and efficiency. This graphic writing then becomes an aesthetic.

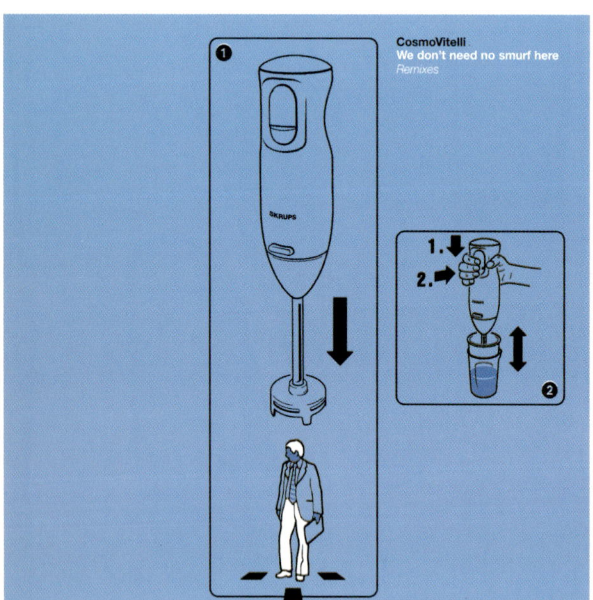

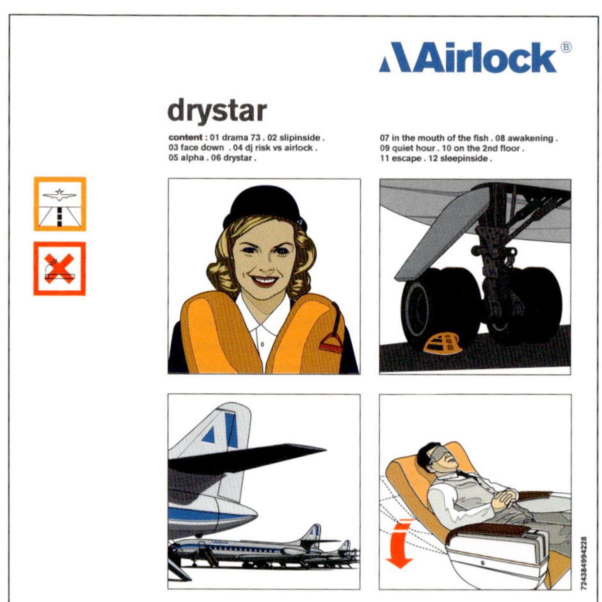

This Page Left)	COSMO VITELLI / WE DON'T NEED NO SMURF HERE REMIXES. CD Single	1999	V2 / DISQUES SOLID
This Page Right)	AIRLOCK / DRYSTAR. CD Album	2001	ONE LITTLE INDIAN
Right Page)	THOMAS DI MATTEO / JAZZ CLICK. EP	2003	MISSIVE

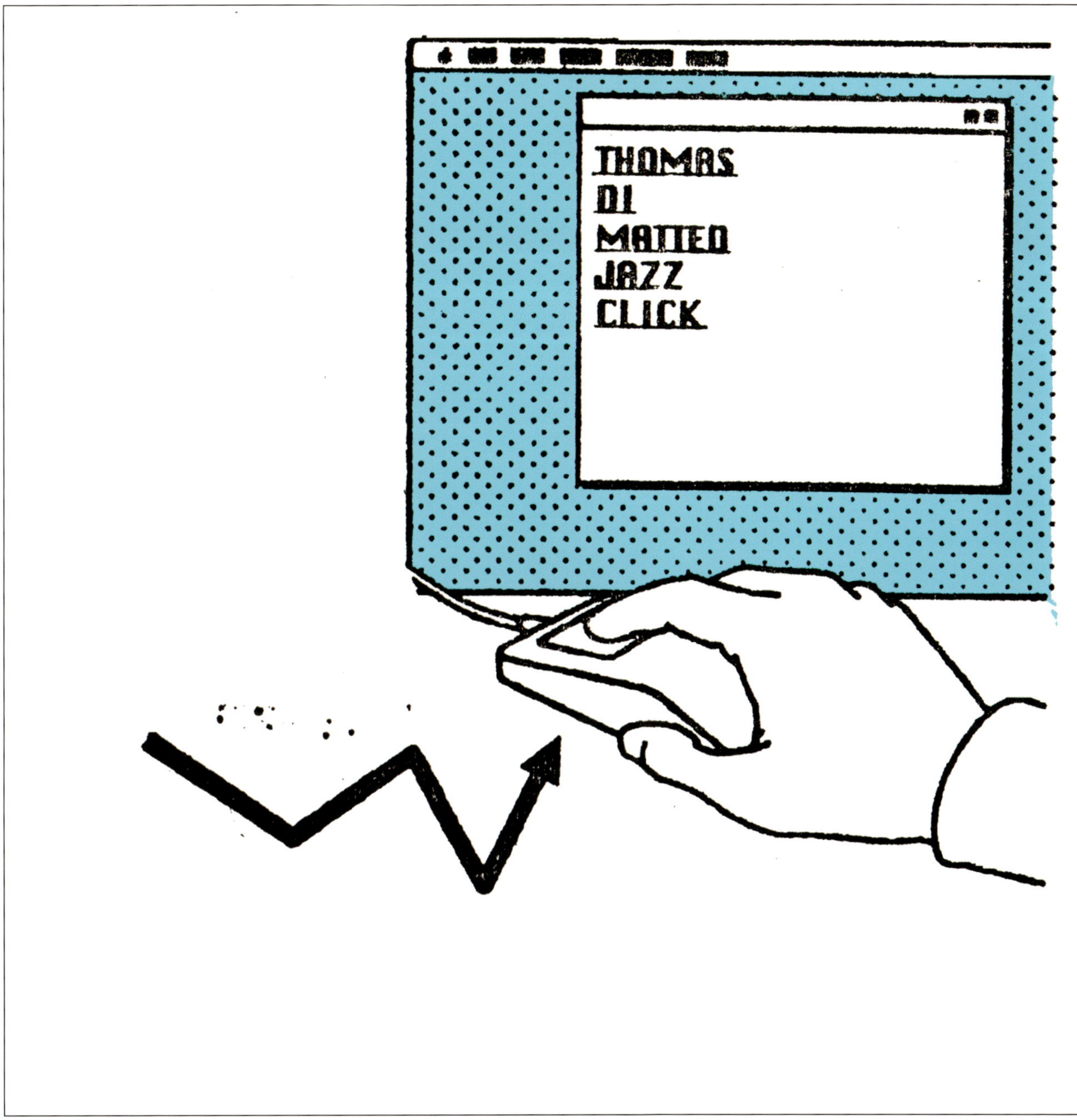
THOMAS
DI
MATTEO
JAZZ
CLICK

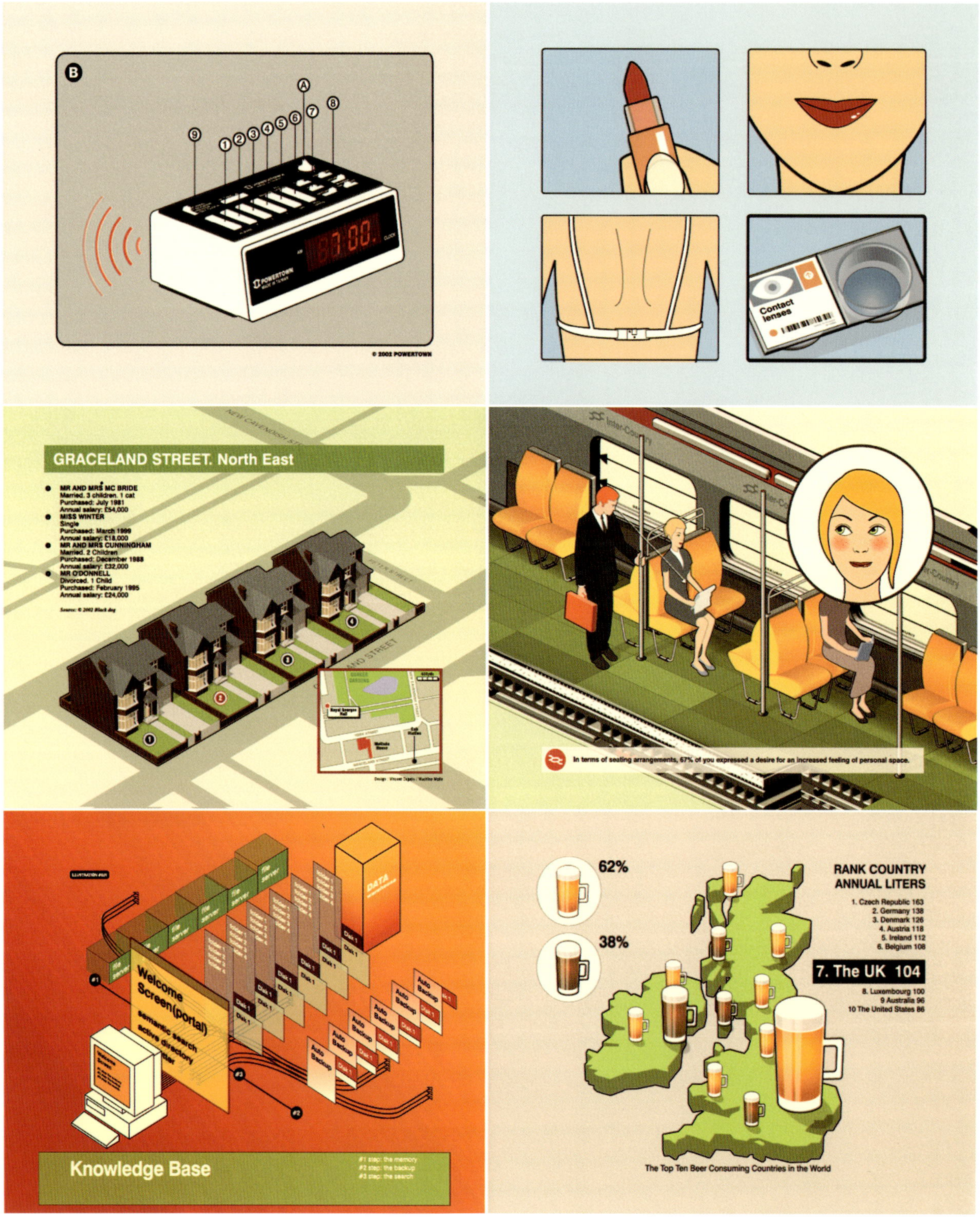

"REMIND ME" BY ROYKSOPP / Video stills from pop-promo

2002

Director: H5
Production: Black Dog Films
Post Production: Machine Molle
Labels: Labels / Wall of Sound

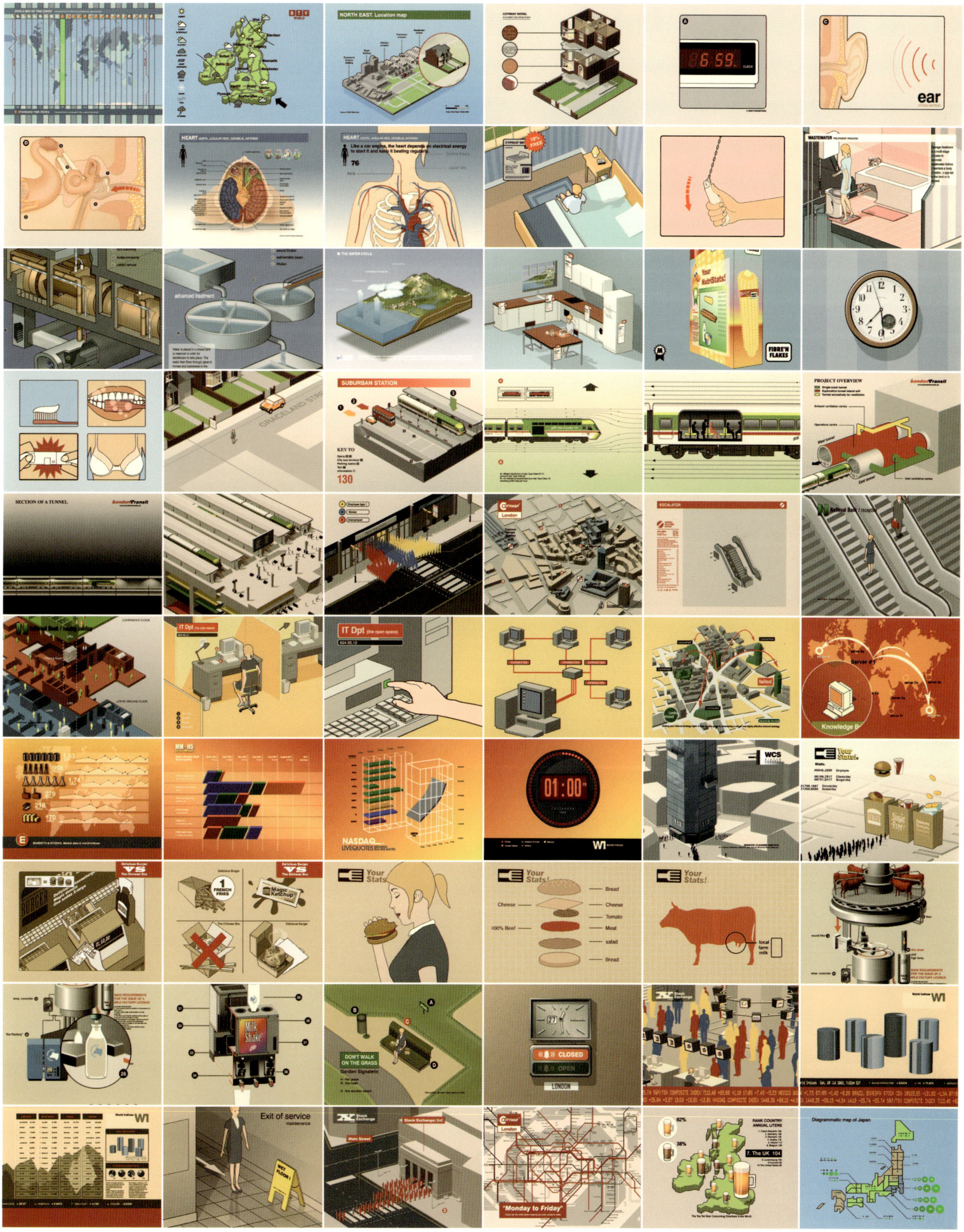
NORTH EAST. Location map
6:59
ear
HEART
advanced treatment
FIBRE'N FLAKES
SUBURBAN STATION
KEY TO
130
PROJECT OVERVIEW
SECTION OF A TUNNEL
ESCALATOR
IT Dpt (the open space)
Knowledge B
NASDAQ
01:00
W1
Your Stats!
FRENCH FRIES
Magic Ketchup
Bread
Cheese
Tomato
Meat
salad
100% Beef
DONT WALK ON THE GRASS
CLOSED
OPEN
LONDON
Milk Shake
Exit of service
WET FLOOR
Main Street
"Monday to Friday"
7. The UK 104
Diagrammatic map of Japan

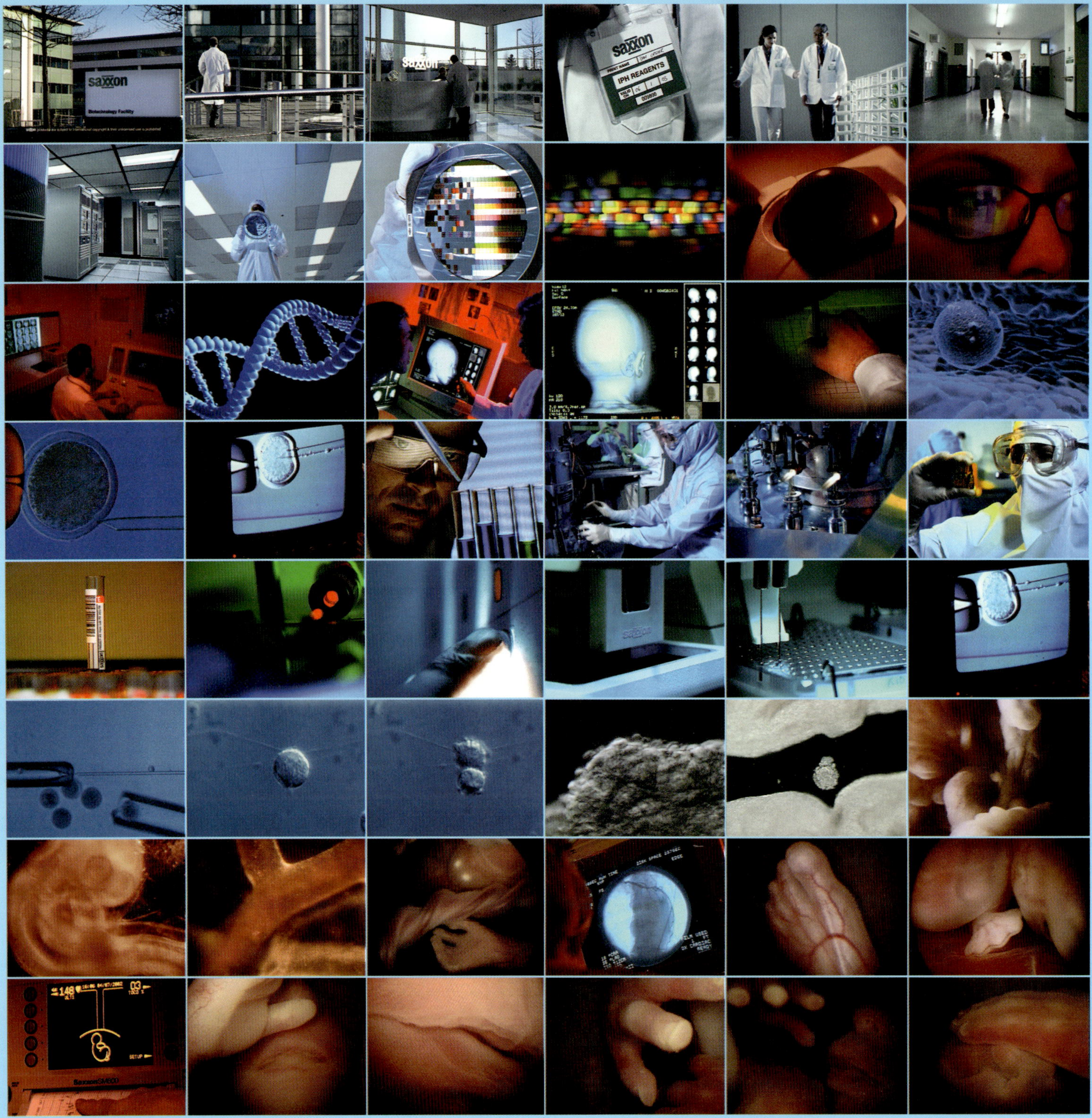
saxxon
IPH REAGENTS

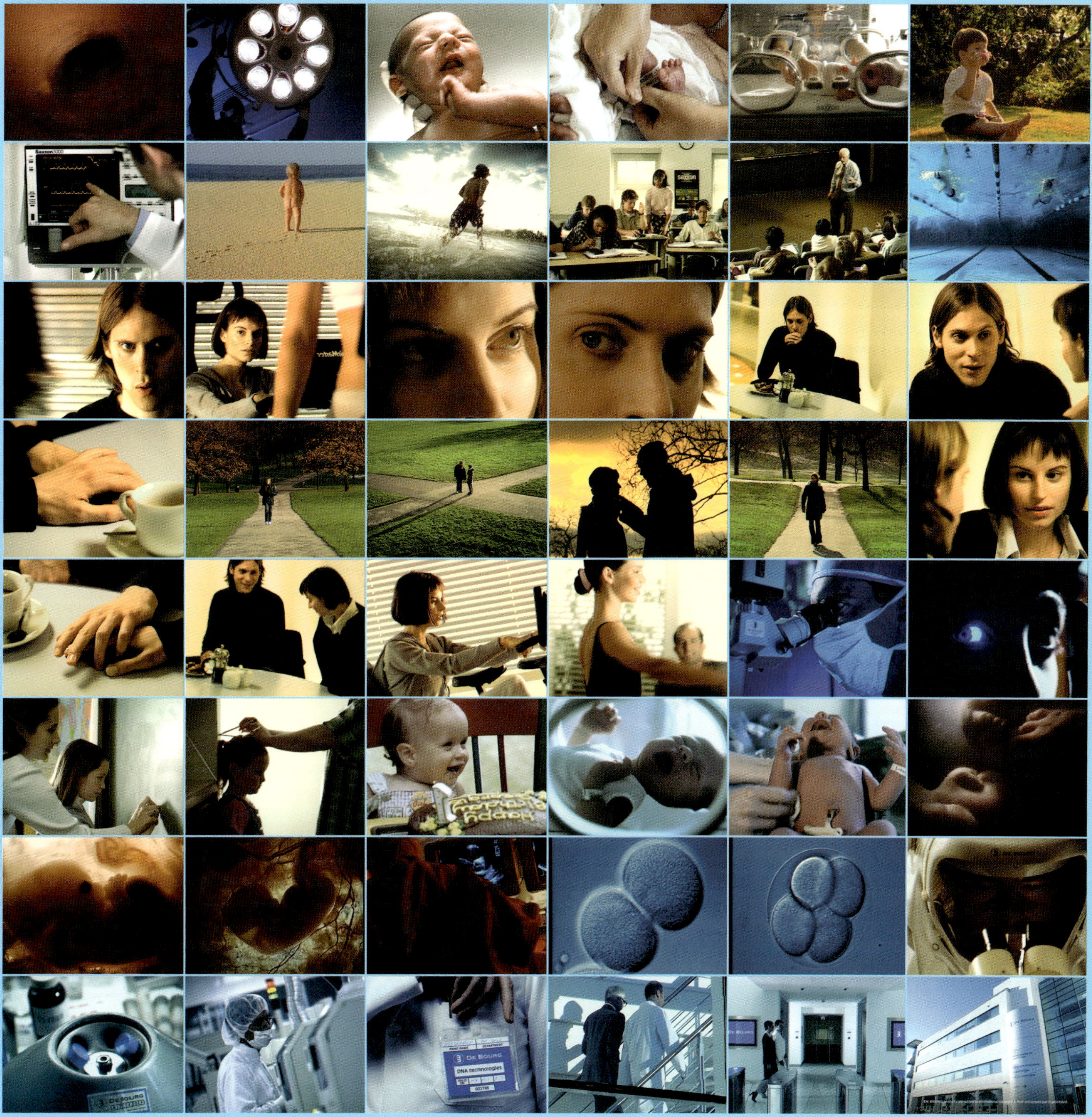

"SPECIAL CASES" BY MASSIVE ATTACK / Video stills from pop-promo 2003

Director: H5
Production: Black Dog Films
Post Production: The Mill
Labels: Virgin UK

CHAPTER 09
WHY TYPOGRAPHY?

なぜタイポグラフィーなのか

答え：古典的なものへの愛着から。説明的あるいは装飾的なものに対する懐疑心から。また「可読性」にこだわるため。

WHY TYPOGRAPHY?

ANSWER: Because of a fondness for classicism; because of a wariness when it comes to the illustrative and the decorative. To concentrate on readability.

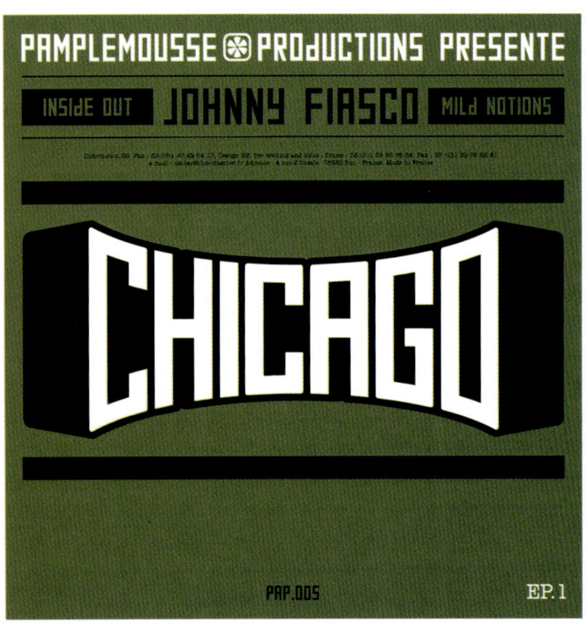

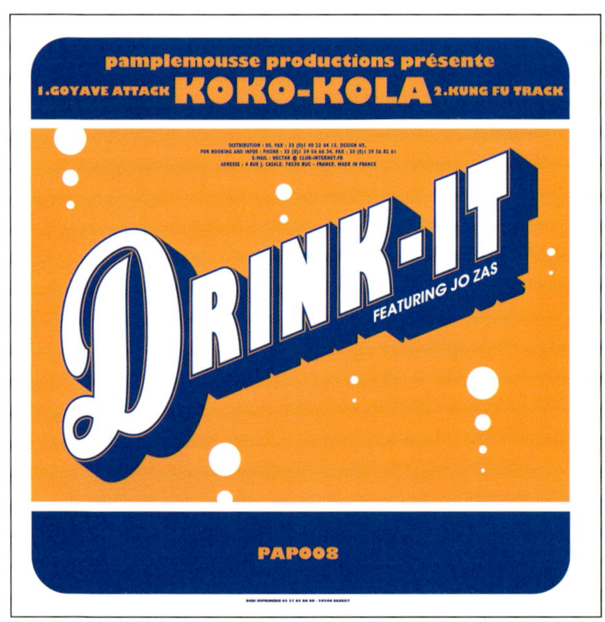

Left Page Left) JOHNNY FIASCO / CHICAGO. EP 1998 PAMPLEMOUSSE
Left Page Right) KOKO KOLA / DRINK IT. EP 1999 PAMPLEMOUSSE
Right Page) BOOGYMANN / EP. EP 1999 PAMPLEMOUSSE

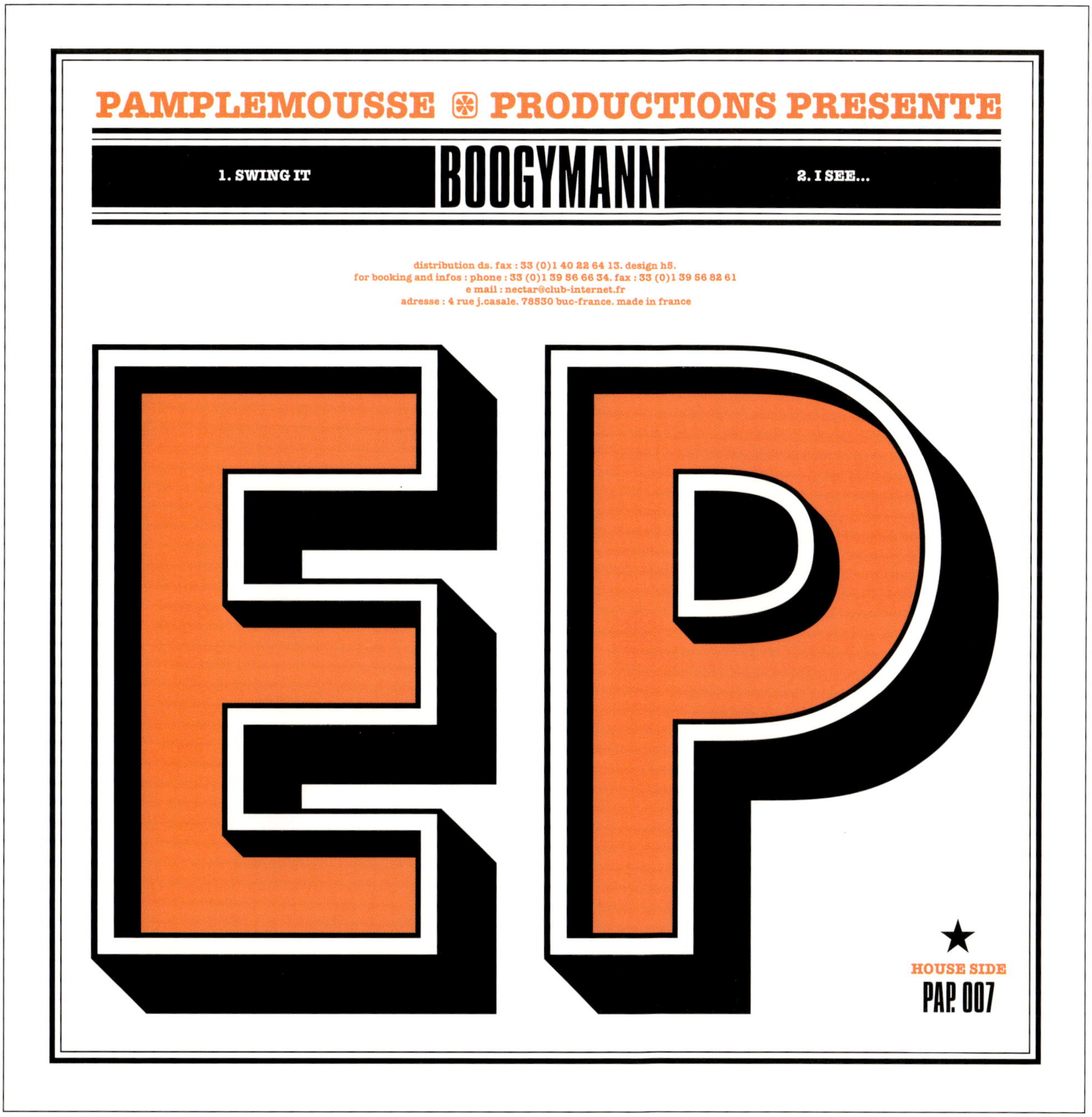
PAMPLEMOUSSE PRODUCTIONS PRESENTE
1. SWING IT
BOOGYMANN
2. I SEE...
distribution ds. fax : 33 (0)1 40 22 64 13. design h5.
for booking and infos : phone : 33 (0)1 39 56 66 34. fax : 33 (0)1 39 56 82 61
e mail : nectar@club-internet.fr
adresse : 4 rue j.casale. 78530 buc-france. made in france
EP
HOUSE SIDE
PAP. 007

SCRATCHED

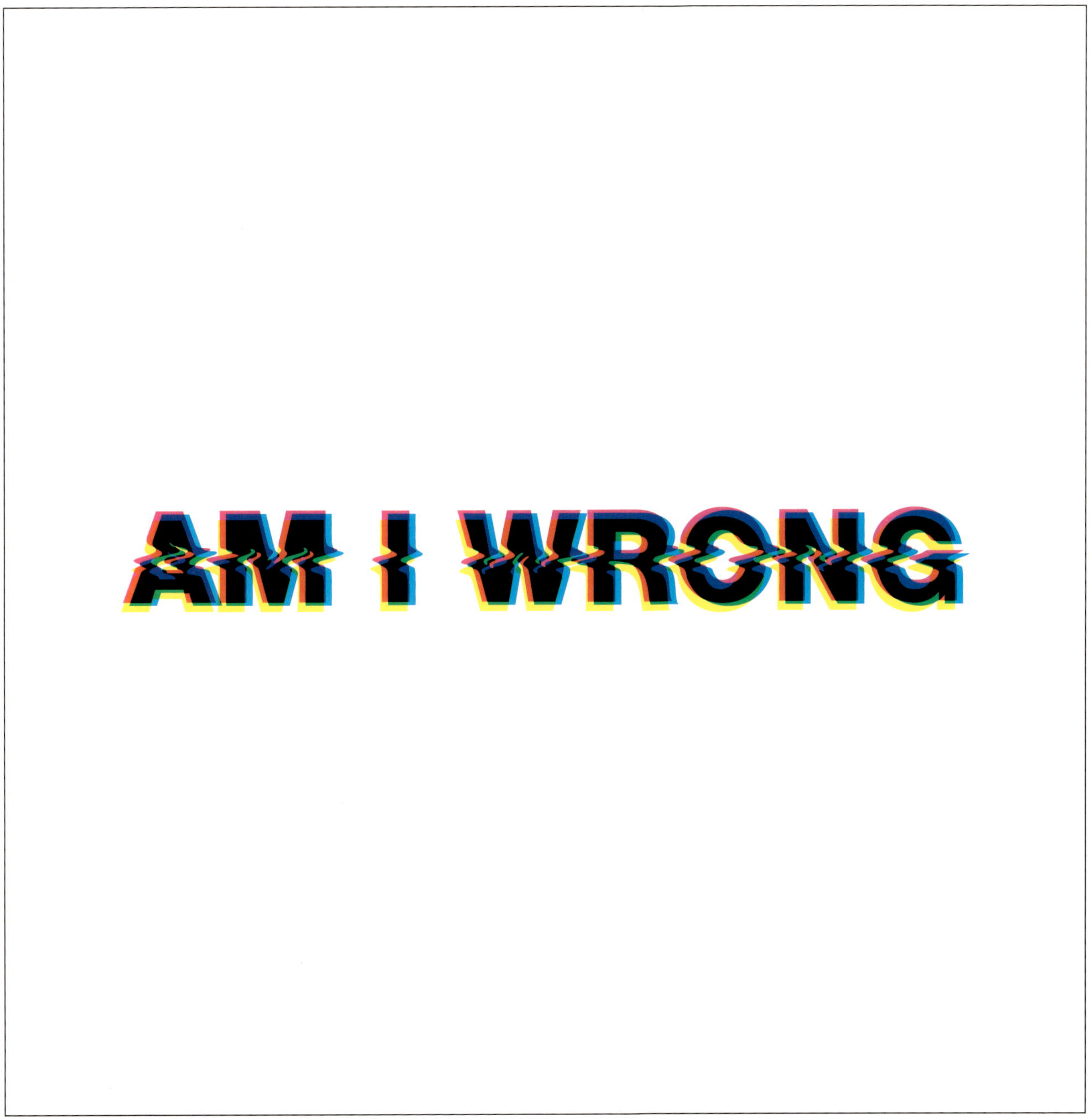

Left Page) ETIENNE DE CRECY / SCRATCHED. EP 2001 V2 / DISQUES SOLID
Right Page) ETIENNE DE CRECY / AM I WRONG. EP 2001 V2 / DISQUES SOLID

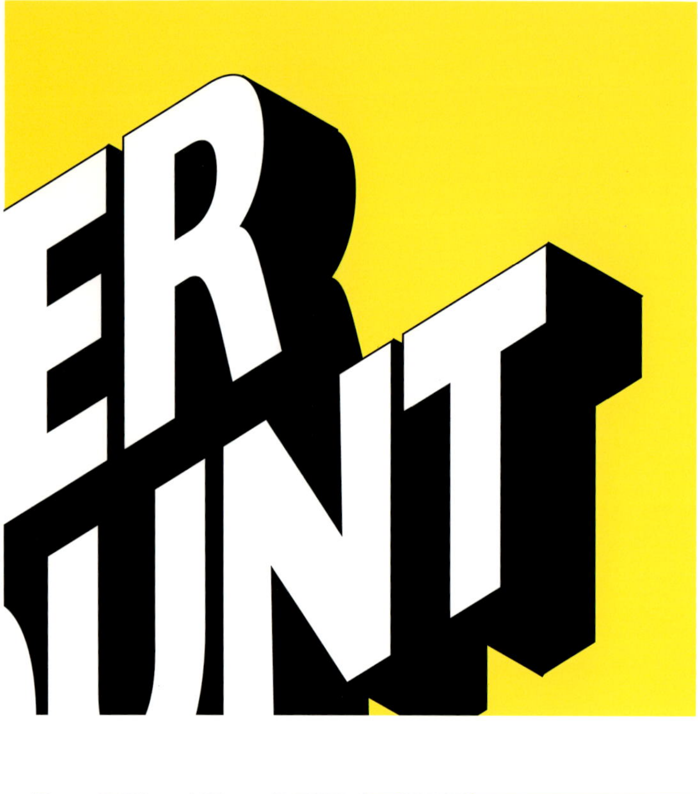

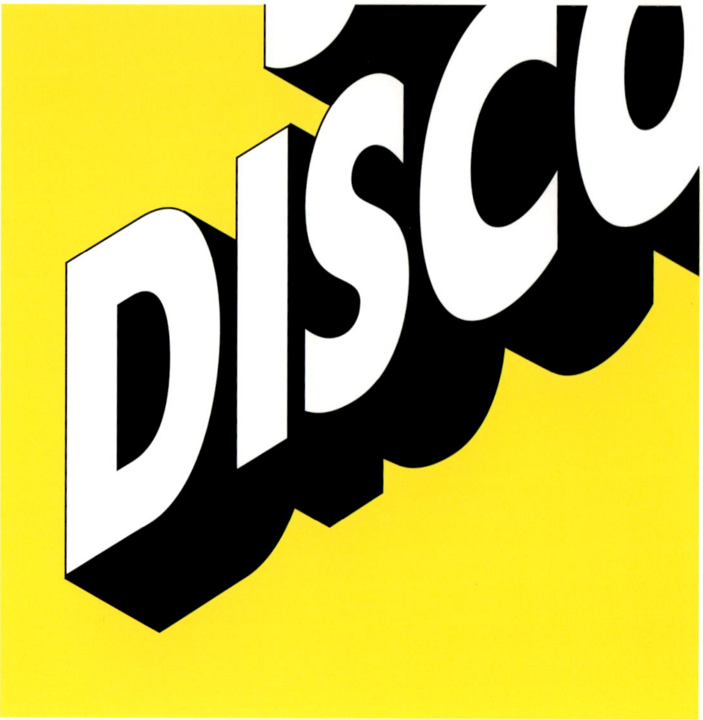

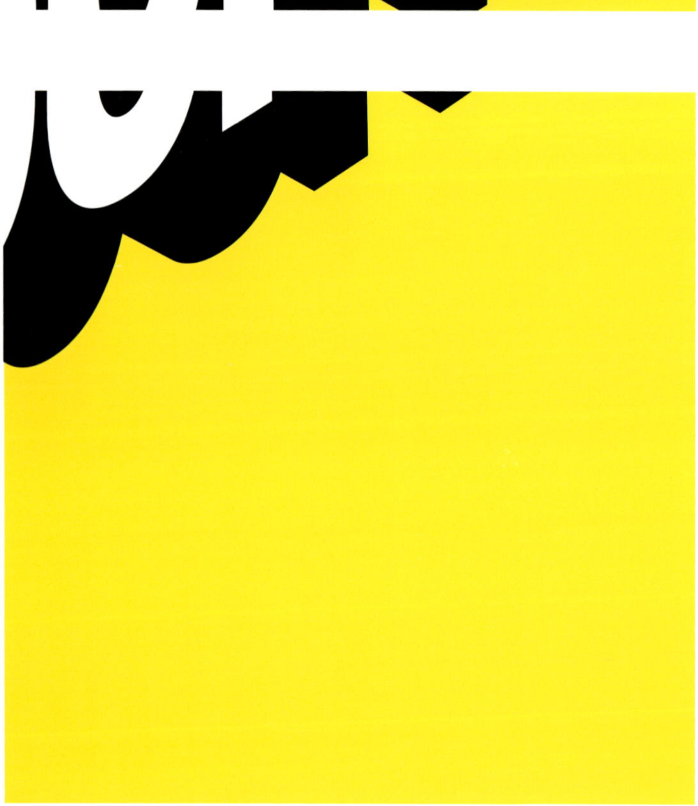

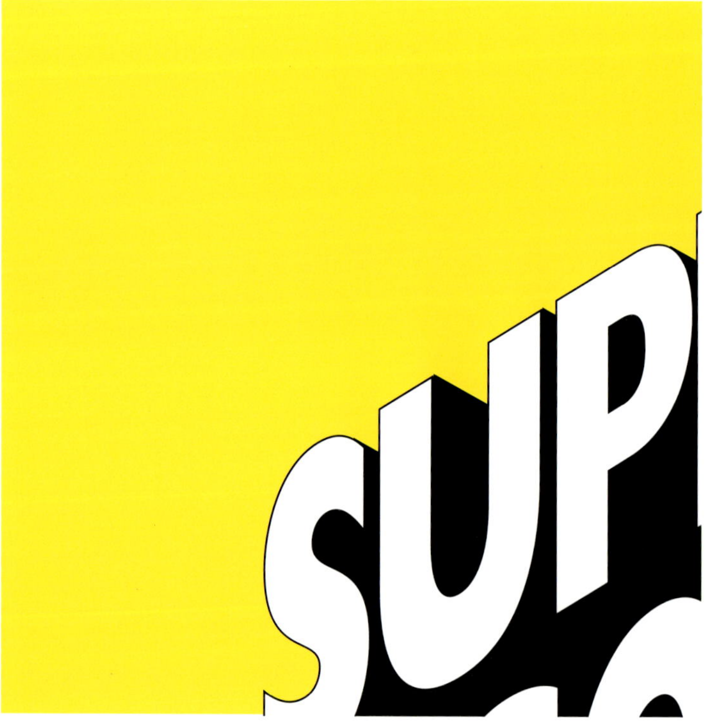

Top Left)	SUPERDISCOUNT/ PART 1. 10"	1996	DISQUES SOLID
Top Right)	SUPERDISCOUNT/ PART 2. 10"	1996	DISQUES SOLID
Bottom Left)	SUPERDISCOUNT/ PART 3. 10"	1996	DISQUES SOLID
Bottom Right)	SUPERDISCOUNT/ PART 4. 10"	1996	DISQUES SOLID

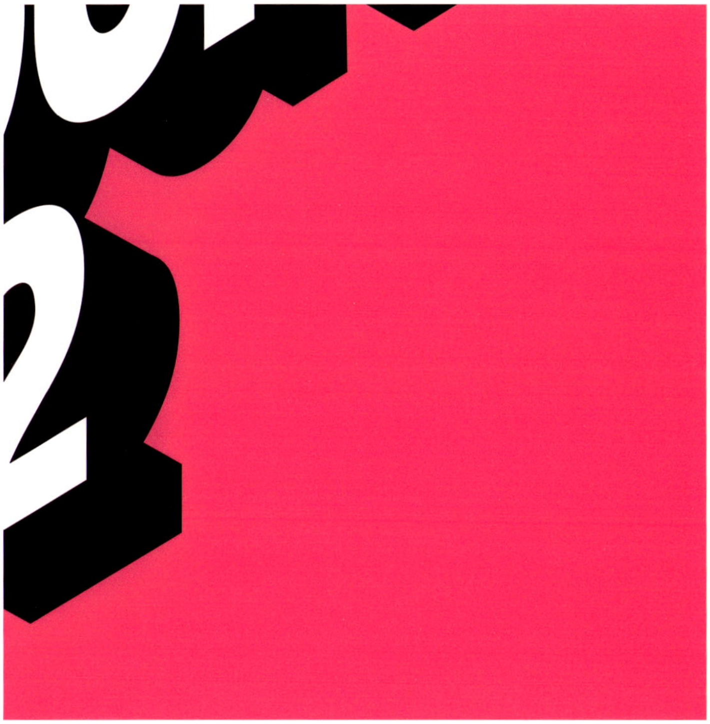

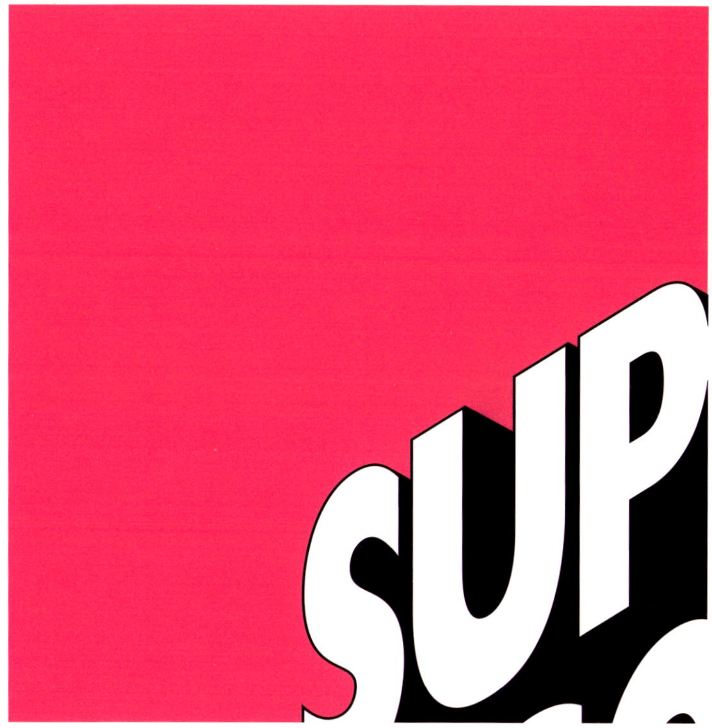

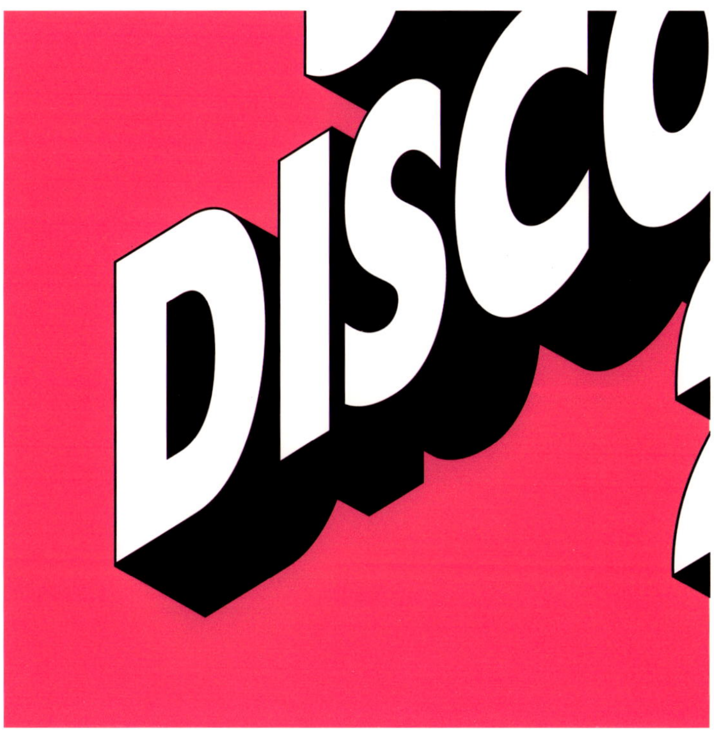

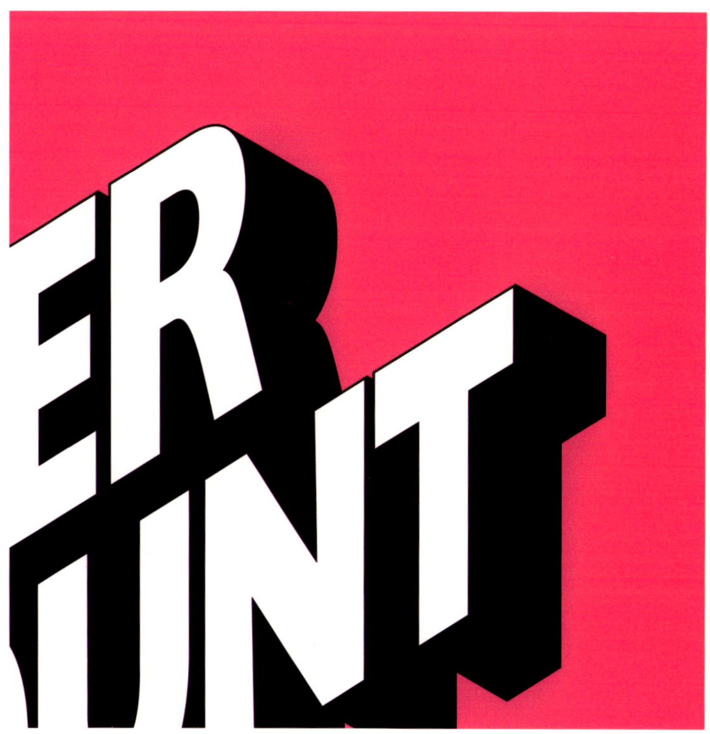

Top Left) SUPERDISCOUNT 2 / PART 1. 10" 2004 PIAS / DISQUES SOLID
Top Right) SUPERDISCOUNT 2 / PART 2. 10" 2004 PIAS / DISQUES SOLID
Bottom Left) SUPERDISCOUNT 3 / PART 1. 10" 2004 PIAS / DISQUES SOLID
Bottom Right) SUPERDISCOUNT 4 / PART 1. 10" 2004 PIAS / DISQUES SOLID

CHOICE / Records Company 1999

ONE SOURCE / Paper Company 1999

OPEN SOUND / Records Company 2000

CONSULTANT / Consulting Agency 2002

BISCUIT MAGAZINE / Magazine 2001

diamondtraxx

DIAMONDTRAXX / Records Company 1998

PÔLE NORD

PÔLE NORD / Records Company 2003

DeNote®
RECORDS

DENOTE / Records Company 2000

Sampling®

SAMPLING / Records Company 2001

MicroMusic®

MICRO MUSIC / Records Company 2002

diamondtraxx

DIAMONDTRAXX / Records Company 1998

PÔLE NORD

PÔLE NORD / Records Company 2003

DeNote®
RECORDS

DENOTE / Records Company 2000

Sampling®

SAMPLING / Records Company 2001

MicroMusic®

MICRO MUSIC / Records Company 2002

Higher energy

DIOR PARFUMS 2003

AZIMUT INDUSTRIES 2002

sterilemind© gallery

STERILEMIND / Art Gallery 2001

WUZ

WUZ / Artist Logotype 2002

SOURCELab

SOURCELAB / Records Company 1996

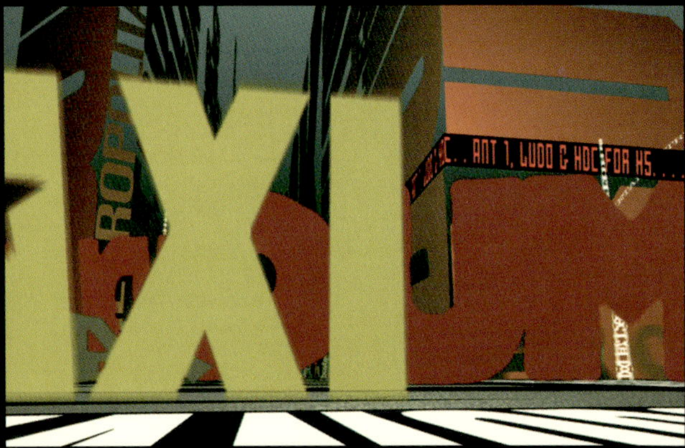
ANT 1, LUDO & HDC FOR H5.

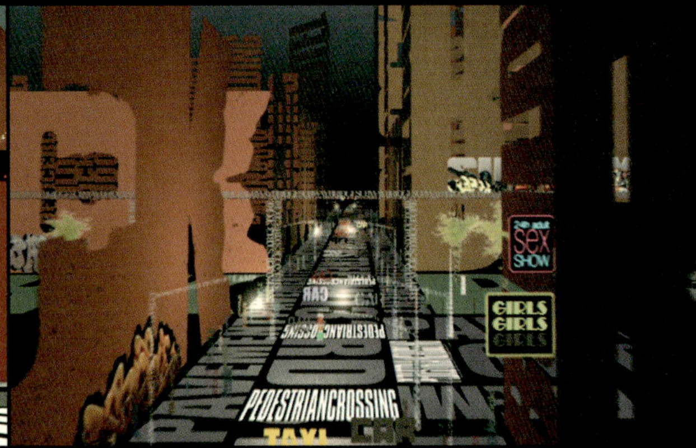
24h adult
sex
SHOW
GIRLS
GIRLS
PEDESTRIANCROSSING
TAXI

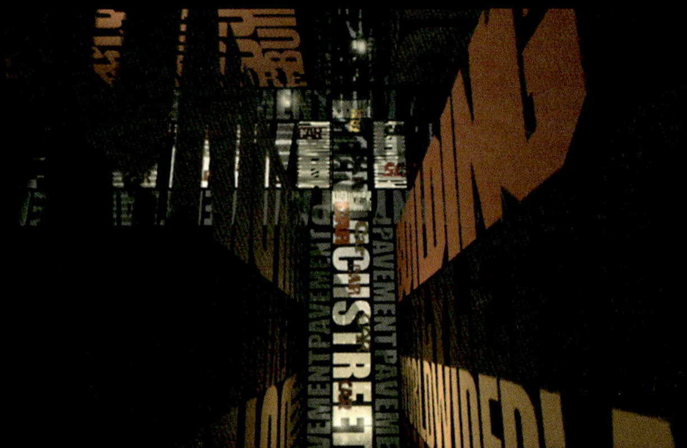
STREET

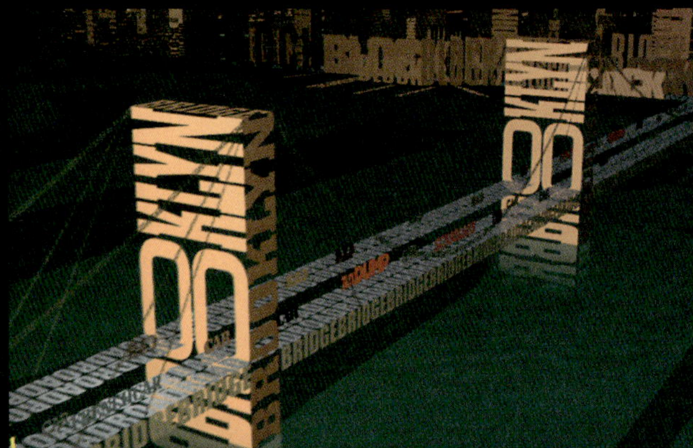
BRIDGEBRIDGE

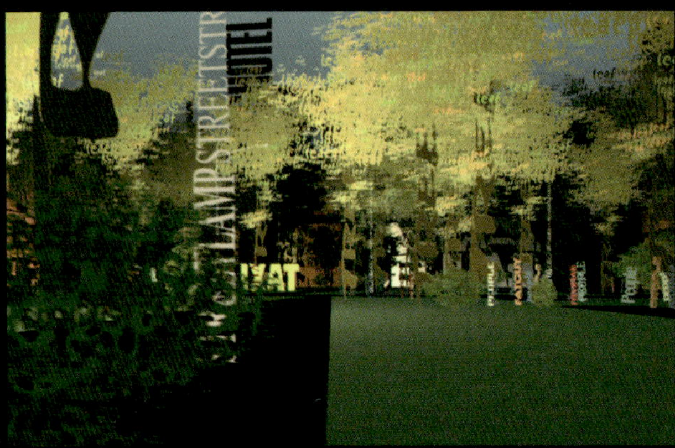
LAMPSTREETSTR

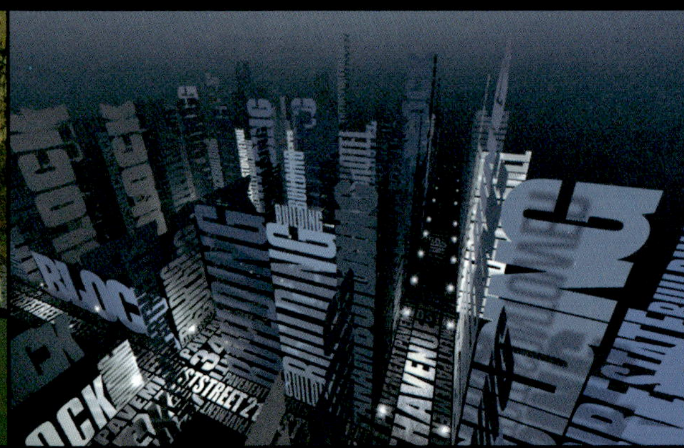

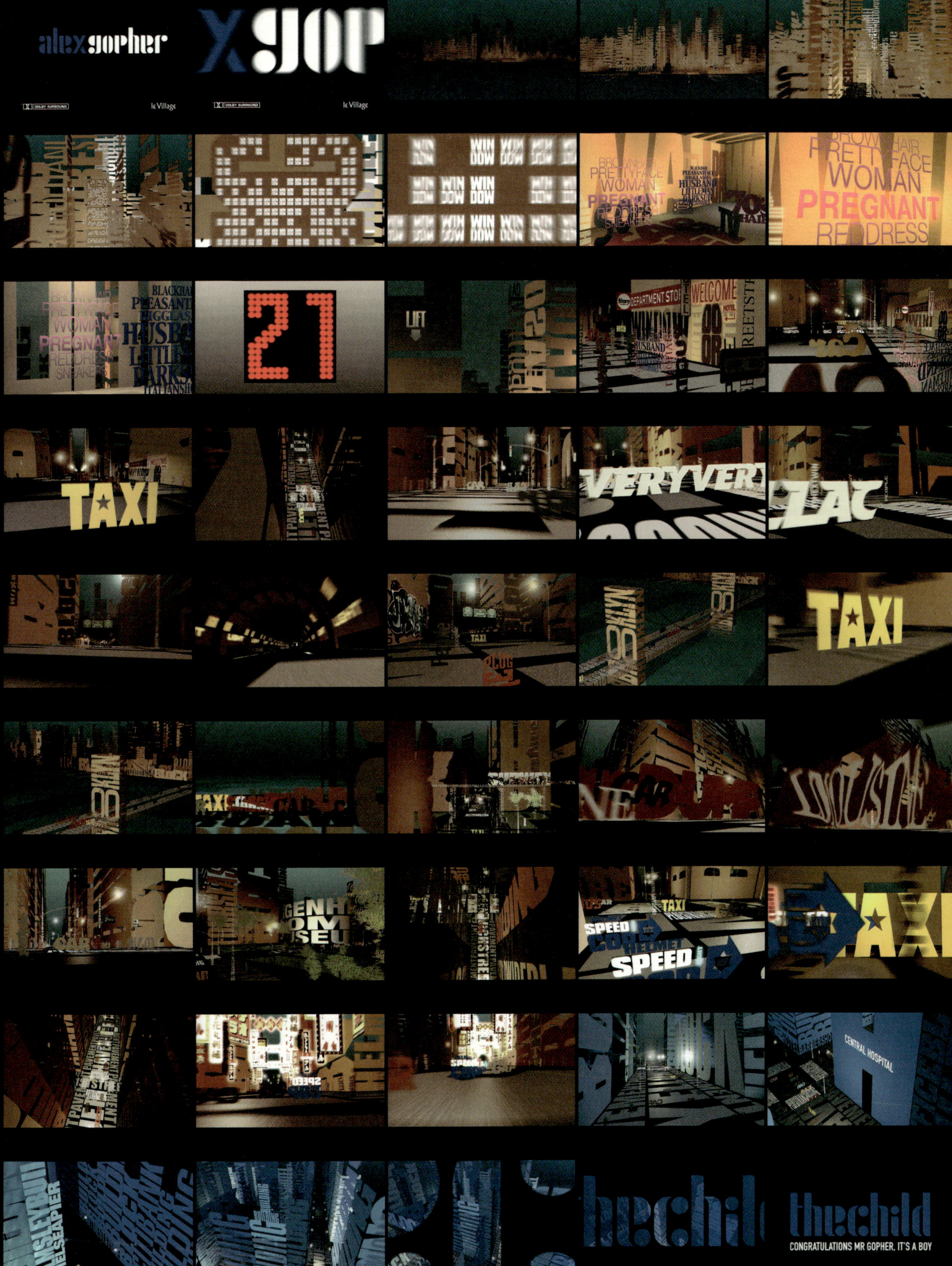
alexgopher
DOLBY SURROUND
le Village
DOLBY SURROUND
le Village
WIN DOW
BROWNHAIR
PRETTYFACE
WOMAN
PREGNANT
REDDRESS
21
LIFT
DEPARTMENT STORE
WELCOME
HUSBAND
TAXI
VERYVERY
TAXI
SPEED
HELMET
SPEED
TAXI
CENTRAL HOSPITAL
BARBERSHOP
thechild
CONGRATULATIONS MR GOPHER, IT'S A BOY

ANSWERS

1 WHEN DO YOU MOST FEEL THE PRESENCE OF « DESIGN » AROUND YOU ?
THE BEST DESIGN IS THE ONE THAT REMAINS HIDDEN

2 WHAT IS YOUR FAVOURITE SHAPE ?
THE CUBE

3 WHAT WAS YOUR HAPPIEST MOMENT IN YOUR WORK EXPERIENCE ?
LE 17 MAI 2002

4 PLEASE LIST UP YOUR 3 FAVOURITE COLOURS
GREY, WHITE AND RED

5 WHAT DO YOU HATE THE MOST ?
TO BELIEVE THAT MONEY IS A GOAL BY ITSELF

6 PLEASE LIST UP YOUR 3 FAVOURITE MATERIALS
DU PAIN, DU FOIE GRAS ET DU CHAMPAGNE

7 WHERE IS YOUR MOST FAVOURITE PLACE
MY BED

8 PLEASE LIST UP YOUR 3 FAVOURITE DESIGNERS
ARNE JACOBSEN, APPLE® &, PAUL RAND

9 PLEASE DEFINE THE WORD « DESIGN »
SIMPLICITY OF THE SHAPE CONSIDERING ITS FUNCTION

10 PLEASE LIST UP YOUR 3 FAVOURITE WORDS
LIBERTÉ, EGALITÉ, FRATERNITÉ

H 25 RUE DU FG POISSONIÈRE 75 009 PARIS FRANCE T + 33 1 42 46 06 33 F + 33 1 42 46 06 23 CONTACT@H5.FR

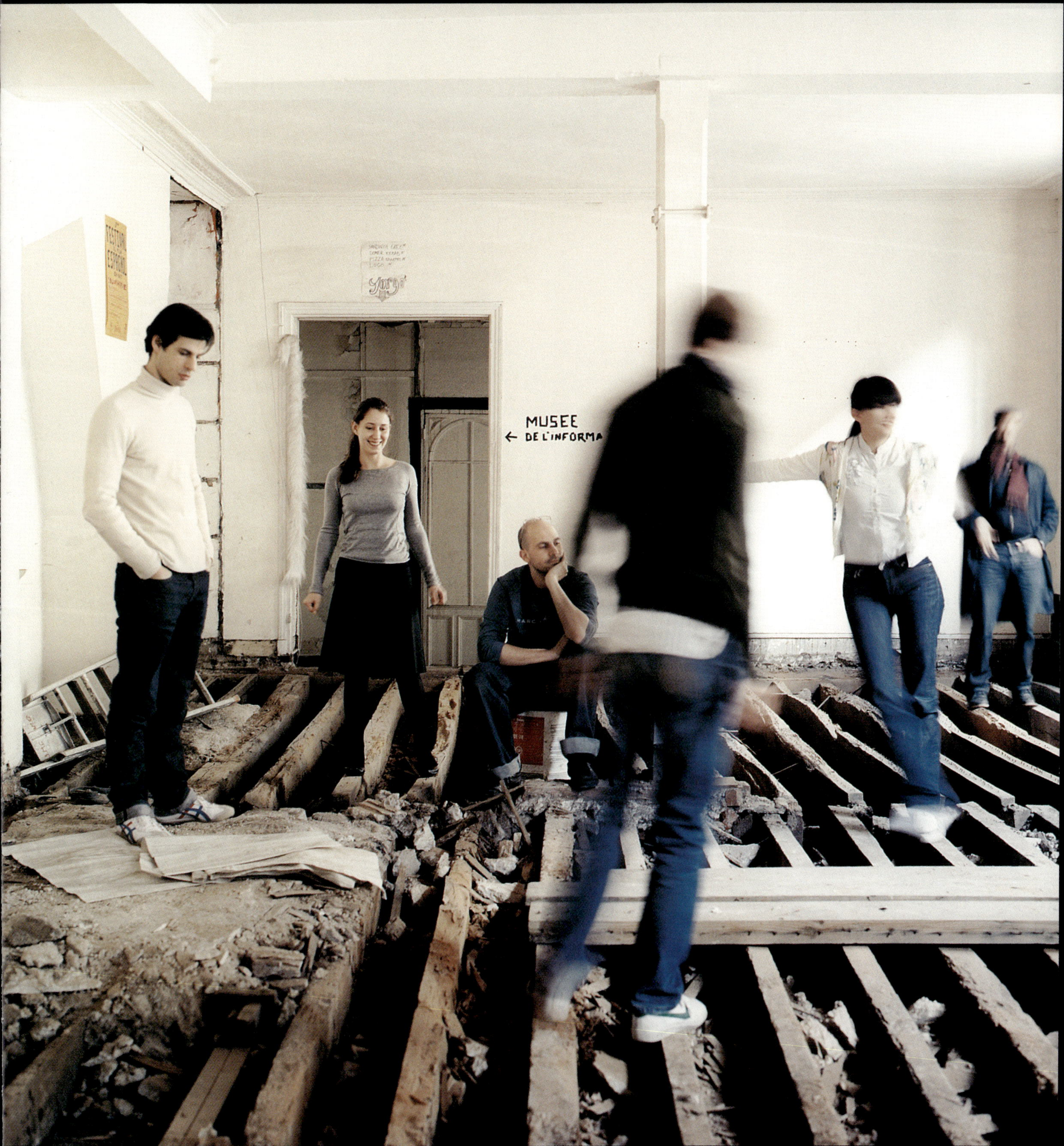
MUSEE
← DE L'INFORMA

EDITORIAL CREDIT

GAS BOOK 18

H5

COVER ARTWORK: H5
CONTRIBUTING EDITOR & TEXT: Angelo Cirimele
STUDIO PHOTO: Cecily Rozier-Chabert

ART DIRECTOR & DESIGN: Ai Fukasawa

PRODUCER & EDITOR: Ayako Terashima
EDITORIAL ASSISTANT: Yumiko Ohchi
TRANSLATOR: Kotaro Motoki

DIRECTOR: Masanori Omae

PUBLISHER: Shinjiro Nishino

Published in Japan in 2005
Gas As Interface Co., Ltd.
3F Claska 1-3-18 Chuocho
Meguro-ku Tokyo 152-0001 Japan
Phone: 81 3 5704 7374 Fax: 81 3 5704 7375
e-mail: contact@gasasif.com
http://www.hellogas.com

ISBN 4-86100-225-7

Printed in Japan by Toppan Printing Co.,Ltd.

First Printing, 2005

GAS BOOK 18
H5
2005年5月21日　初版第一刷発行

発行者　西野慎二郎
印刷所　凸版印刷株式会社
発行所　ガスアズインターフェイス株式会社
発売　株式会社ビー・エヌ・エヌ新社
http://www.bnn.co.jp
〒163-1111　東京都新宿区西新宿6-22-1　新宿スクエアタワー11階
TEL: 03 5339 3889　FAX: 03 3345 1127

ISBN 4-86100-225-7

PAGE **62 AND 63**

質問	回答
01) 身の周りで最もデザインを感じる時は？	最高なデザインは目立たないところにある。
02) 好きなフォルムは？	キューブ。
03) 今後／以前の制作活動で一番嬉しい／嬉しかった瞬間は？	２００２年５月１７日。
04) 好きなカラーを順番に３つ／４つ並べて下さい。	グレイ、白、赤。
05) 嫌いな事は？	お金が全てと思うこと。
06) 好きなマテリアルを３つ答えて下さい。	パン、フォアグラ、シャンパン。
07) あなたが一番好きな場所は？	自分のベッド。
08) 好きなデザイナーを３人上げてください。	アルネ・ヤコブセン、アップル®、ポール・ランド。
09) あなたにとってアート／デザインとは？	機能を考慮したシンプルなかたち。
10) 好きな言葉を３つ教えて下さい。	Liberté、Egalité、Fraternité（訳：自由、平等、博愛）。

STUDIO

Photo: Cecily Rozier-Chabert